Abraham Lincoln

Abraham Lincoln

The Observations of
John G. Nicolay
and
John Hay

Edited by Michael Burlingame

Southern Illinois University Press / Carbondale

10 09 08 07   4 3 2 1

Library of Congress Cataloging-in-Publication Data
Abraham Lincoln : the observations of John G. Nicolay
and John Hay / edited by Michael Burlingame
     p. cm.
Includes bibliographical references and index.
ISBN-13: 978-0-8093-2738-6 (cloth : alk. paper)
ISBN-10: 0-8093-2738-4 (cloth : alk. paper)
1. Lincoln, Abraham, 1809–1865—Anecdotes.
2. Presidents—United States—Biography—Anecdotes.
3. United States—Politics and government—1861–
1865—Anecdotes. 4. United States—History—Civil
War, 1861–1865—Anecdotes. 5. Lincoln, Abraham,
1809–1865—Friends and associates—Anecdotes.
I. Burlingame, Michael, 1941– II. Nicolay, John G.
(John George), 1832–1901. III. Hay, John, 1838–1905.
E457.15.A155 2007
973.7092—dc22   2006017973

Printed on recycled paper. ♻

For Lois

CONTENTS

PREFACE

Abraham Lincoln: A History by Lincoln's White House secretaries John G. Nicolay and John Hay, though flawed in many ways, contains invaluable passages based on their own personal observations in Washington. As they noted in the introduction to their ten-volume *magnum opus*, "We were the daily and nightly witnesses of the incidents, the anxieties, the fears, and the hopes which pervaded the Executive Mansion and the National Capital. The President's correspondence, both official and private, passed through our hands; he gave us his full confidence. We had personal acquaintance and daily official intercourse with Cabinet Officers, Members of Congress, Governors, and Military and Naval Officers of all grades, whose affairs brought them to the White House."[1] Vivid descriptions, buried amid chapters of outmoded history that Hay himself called "dull," are excerpted here.[2] Few modern readers have the patience to wade through 4,709 pages in search of such reminiscences. The present volume complements the five volumes of diaries, letters, memoranda, journalism, and selected writings by Nicolay and Hay previously issued by the Southern Illinois University Press.

Also included here are some passages from the biography in which the authors interpret their boss's character, actions, and fame. These may reflect Lincoln's own thinking about the matters discussed.

The excerpts are primarily taken from the volumes covering the first half of Lincoln's presidency, when Hay made only sporadic entries in his diary. The firsthand accounts in the volumes covering the second half of Lincoln's presidency come mainly from that diary, which is much more complete than it was for 1861 and 1862.

The introduction, a slightly altered form of "Nicolay and Hay: Court Historians" (*Journal of the Abraham Lincoln Association*, vol. 19, no. 1 [winter 1998]: 1–20), describes the composition, reception, and reputation of the biography.

Abraham Lincoln

INTRODUCTION

$\mathcal{W}$hen John G. Nicolay and John Hay published excerpts from their biography of Lincoln in the *Century Magazine* starting in 1886, some readers found the balance between historical background and biographical foreground risibly lopsided.[1] One commentator, who had "a very great interest in Lincoln" and was "disappointed at finding so little concerning him," declared, "The *Century* for March continues its biographical remarks on the great men of Abraham Lincoln's time, with a few bits of irrelevancy about Lincoln himself thrown in. The historical narrative that Messrs. Hay and Nicolay are giving us is a great success as a picture of days gone by, and it is a great pity that it should be marred by those personal details of an obscure Illinois lawyer which we notice have crept into the story from time to time." This puckish reviewer complained that the title of Nicolay and Hay's work constituted false advertising: "We sometimes feel discouraged over the tendency our literary men have to misname their works. 'Abraham Lincoln,' by Messrs. Nicolay and Hay, would properly be christened 'From Boone to Booth; or, the Surprising Adventures of Senator Tom, Governor Dick, and Congressman Harry, in the Early Days of the Roaring Republic.'"[2] Two months later this same reviewer cautioned readers that "the picture of the Pharaohs in the last *Century* must not be mistaken for illustrations in the 'Life of Lincoln.' The authors of that exhaustive biography passed the Pharaohs several numbers back, and are understood to be well along in their retrospective summary of the Middle Ages."[3]

It was a legitimate complaint. As Harry E. Pratt noted, the ten-volume work has been "justly criticized as more of a history of the Civil War than a life of Lincoln."[4] At one point, Lincoln virtually disappears from view for 395 pages as the authors give what their editor, Richard Watson Gilder, called "the secret history of the secession conspiracy."[5] One of Hay's biographers rightly observed that at times "the narrative, instead of flowing forward like a river, seems to stagnate in a lagoon or to lose itself in some subterranean channel," and thus the book is more "an historical quarry or encyclopedia" than a true biography.[6] Another Hay biographer thought the title *Abraham Lincoln: A Chronicle* would have been better" than *Abraham Lincoln: A History*.[7]

Contemporaries also protested against the unabashedly partisan tone of the biography, which at times reads like a 1.5 million–word Republican campaign tract. Nicolay and Hay waved the bloody shirt vigorously, portraying Democrats as vicious traitors, while at the same time fulsomely defending every action of the Grand Old Party. Hay frankly referred to the biography as a "ponderous Republican history."[8] Augustus St. Gaudens, a vast admirer of Lincoln, complained of the Nicolay and Hay biography as it appeared month after month in the *Century*: "How damn partizan it's getting!" He disliked all the "pitching in, calling names, etc."[9] Even Gilder, the authors' enthusiastic editor, tempered his extravagant praise of the work by noting, "Your sanction of right and natural indignation at wrong sometimes injures the necessary philosophical equipoise."[10] Gilder warned Nicolay and Hay that "partisanship has been charged, and doubtless will be charged. . . . It may be that future historians, and critics of history, will be less severe in the judgment of some you have thought it right to condemn."[11]

The most conspicuous victim of their condemnation was George B. McClellan, whom Hay eviscerated in his chapters on the Army of the Potomac. To Nicolay, Hay confided, "I have toiled and labored through ten chapters over him (McC). I think I have left the impression of his mutinous imbecility, and I have done it in a perfectly courteous manner. . . . It is of the utmost moment that we should *seem* fair to him, while we are destroying him."[12] In discussing the failure of McClellan to come to General John Pope's assistance at the second battle of Bull Run, Hay declared, "McClellan['s] . . . conduct from beginning to end can only be condemned."[13] At the close of those chapters Hay bluntly concluded that "the candid historian of the future will have no sentiment but wonder when he comes to tell the story of his long mismanagement of a great, brave, and devoted army, backed by a Government which strained every nerve to support him, and by a people whose fiery zeal would have made him the idol of the nation if he had given them the successes which their sacrifices deserved, and which were a dozen times within his grasp."[14] (This judgment, it should be noted, resembles that of McClellan's most judicious biographer, Stephen W. Sears, who contended that his subject was "inarguably the worst" general to lead the Army of the Potomac.)[15]

Publicly, Nicolay and Hay did not acknowledge their partisanship. In the introduction to their biography, they emphatically asserted that they were impartial:

> We claim for our work that we have devoted to it twenty years of almost unremitting assiduity; that we have neglected no means in our power to ascertain the truth; that we have rejected no authentic facts essential to a candid story; that we have had no theory to establish, no personal grudge to gratify, no unavowed objects to subserve. We have aimed to write a sufficiently full and absolutely honest history of a great man and a great time; and . . . we claim that there is not a line in all these volumes dictated by malice or unfairness. . . . If we gained nothing else by our long association with Mr. Lincoln we hope at least that we acquired from him the habit of judging men and events with candor and impartiality. The material placed in our hands was unexampled in value and fullness; we have felt the obligation of using

it with perfect fairness. We have striven to be equally just to friends and to adversaries; where the facts favor our enemies we have recorded them ungrudgingly; where they bear severely upon statesmen and generals whom we have loved and honored we have not scrupled to set them forth, at the risk of being accused of coldness and ingratitude to those whom we have lived on terms of intimate friendship.[16]

Privately, Nicolay rejected charges of partisanship, declaring that "we stand in no awe of them. We deny that it is partisanship to use the multiplication table, reverence the Decalogue, or obey the Constitution of the United States. When logic, morals and law all unite to condemn the secession and rebellion of 1861, he will be a rash critic to pronounce censure upon any who helped put down that secession and rebellion, or who venture truthfully to record its incidents."[17] When in 1881 Nicolay published a short book, *The Outbreak of Rebellion*,[18] that was criticized for its partisanship, Hay told him, "All the reviews acknowledged its merits of style, accuracy, and readableness—but nearly everyone objected to its tone of aggressive Northernism. This was a surprise to me. I read it in MS. and thought it perfectly fair and candid—but I am of that age, and imbued with all its prejudices."[19]

In fact "aggressive Northernism" characterizes *Abraham Lincoln: A History*, which described as "absurdly insignificant" the grievances cited to justify secession and deplored the "barbarous" conduct of the "traitors" and "conspirators" who dragged the cotton states out of the Union.[20] The authors ridiculed Governor William H. Gist's message to the South Carolina legislature for resting on an "absurd contradiction in terms."[21] At the close of their lengthy history of the secession movement, they sermonized thus:

> In ages happily past, the anger of a king, the caprice of a mistress, or the ambition of a minister has often deluged a nation in blood. But in our day the conscience of civilization demands that the sword shall only defend the life of governments, and the life, liberty, and property

4

of their subjects. It has ordained that written constitutions shall decide claims of rulers and rights of citizens. Casuistry the most adroit could not prove the right of free States to expel the slave States for believing the institution of slavery to be a substantial blessing; equally absurd was the doctrine that slave States had a right to destroy the Union by secession because the free States thought slavery a moral, social, and political evil.[22]

In passages like this, Nicolay and Hay regressed to their earlier days as editorial writers. Hay told Nicolay that when composing their biography they must strike a balance between sternness and indulgence:

> We must not show ourselves to the public in the attitude of two old dotards fighting over again the politics of their youth. . . . We must not write a stump speech in eight vols. . . . We will not fall in with the present tone of blubbering sentiment, of course. But we ought to write the history of those times like two everlasting angels—who know everything, judge everything, tell the truth ab[ou]t everything and don't care a twang of their harps about one side or the other. There will be one exception. We are Lincoln men all the way through. But in other little matters, let us look at men as insects and not blame the black beetle because he is not a grasshopper.[23]

Abraham Lincoln: A History bristles with editorial asides reflecting the authors' laissez-faire ideology. In his discussion of the massive Illinois internal improvements scheme of the 1830s, Hay declared, "It was too much to expect of the Illinois Legislature . . . that it should understand that the best thing it could do to forward this prosperous tendency of things was to do nothing; for this is a lesson which has not yet been learned by any legislature in the world."[24] The hostility to socialism that formed the core of Hay's novel *The Bread-Winners* creeps into the Lincoln biography. Speaking of Chief Black Hawk, Hay observed, "He had come to believe that he had been foully wronged by the treaty which was his own act; he had even convinced himself that 'land cannot be sold,' a proposition in political economy which our modern socialists would be puzzled to accept or confute."[25]

If some contemporaries objected to Nicolay and Hay's partisanship, others wondered if they had tailored their story to please Robert Todd Lincoln, who, it was believed, pressured the biographers to paint a flattering portrait of his father and other members of the family. Lincoln's longtime law partner, William H. Herndon, harbored such suspicions: Nicolay and Hay "handle things with silken gloves and 'a camel-hair pencil,'" Herndon protested; "they do not write with an iron pen." They were "writing the life of Lincoln under the surveillance of 'Bob' Lincoln." Nicolay and Hay, Herndon guessed, "are afraid of Bob; he gives them materials and they in their turn play *hush*."[26] Milton Hay, a lawyer who had known Lincoln well in Springfield, chided his nephew John for being too solicitous of Robert Todd Lincoln's sensibilities. After reading the account of Lincoln's broken engagement with Mary Todd, Milton Hay told John, "I think the explanation of his [Lincoln's] morbidity about his contemplated marriage would have been easier for you but for your regard for Rob[er]t Lincoln's feelings."[27]

In fact, Robert Todd Lincoln was, as David C. Mearns put it, the "silent partner" in the composition of *Abraham Lincoln: A History*.[28] The authors did not dare offend Robert, who controlled access to his father's voluminous papers. They ran the greatest risk of offense while chronicling the story of Lincoln's early life, which was Hay's assignment. In 1884, Hay told Robert that "every line has been written in a spirit of reverence and regard." But, he added, "you may find here and there words or sentences which do not suit you. I write you now to request that you will read with a pencil in your hand and strike out everything to which you object. I will adopt your view in all cases whether I agree with it or not, but I cannot help hoping that you will find nothing objectionable."[29] Robert accepted this invitation to wield his blue pencil, which he used to strike out several passages reflecting poorly on his grandfather, Thomas Lincoln, and one that he thought did no credit to his father. The complete manuscript of the biography is not extant, but from fragments preserved at the Lincoln Presidential Library and at Brown University, we can learn what upset him. Robert objected most strenuously to Hay's depiction of Thomas Lincoln. Hay told Gilder, "The only weak link in the chain is Tom Lincoln—but I can't dwell on that. His grandson is extremely sensitive about it. It is not an ignoble feeling in R. T. L. He says 'he feels sorry for the old man, and does not think it right to jump on him, in the broad light of his son's fame.'"[30] (Recent scholarship suggests that Hay's view of Thomas Lincoln was accurate.)[31] The italicized portions of the following excerpts from the first chapter were cut by Hay at Robert's request:

> Thomas, to whom were reserved the honors of an illustrious paternity, *appears never to have done any[thing] else especially deserving of mention. He was an idle, roving, inefficient, good natured man, as the son of a widow is apt to be according to the Spanish proverb. He had no vices so far as we can learn but he also had no virtues to speak of.* He learned the trade of a carpenter *but accomplished little of it.* . . . he seems to have resembled his son in appearance. *Men like him may be seen every day in Western rural towns, fond of story-telling, of talking things over by the red-hot stove in tavern bar-rooms, or in the cool door ways of livery stables, according to the season. He was a Jackson Democrat, as those of his kind usually were. He was discursive in his religious affiliations, changing his church about as often as he changed his residence, but died a member of the Disciples or "Campbellite" Baptist Church.* . . . It required full as earnest and intelligent industry to persuade a living out of those barren hillocks, and weedy hollows covered with stunted and scrubby underbrush, as it would amid the rocks and sands of the Northern coast. *But neither the will nor the intelligence was there.* . . . Four years later, *the unlucky farmer seemed about to belie his baleful reputation, for by one of those spasmodic efforts not unknown to men inherently indolent,* he purchased *without money as usual though not without price* a fine farm.

. . . The title, however, remained in him only a little while, *and the spurt of enterprise died away into the habitual languor of the man,* and after his property had passed out of his control, he *betook himself to the last resort of restless inefficiency, and* looked about for another place where he owed no debts and could get fresh land for little or nothing.

Hay eliminated similar passages in the second chapter of the first draft.[32] The following sentences were struck from what appears to be a later draft of the first chapter: "After the lapse of one hundred years, the standing of the [Lincoln] family is on the whole far below what it was at the Declaration of Independence. The President seems to have concentrated in himself the genius and virtue of all his race." [33] Also cut from this draft was Lincoln's own account of sewing shut the eyes of balky hogs.[34]

Hay promised to change the text to please Robert: "I will do what you suggest in final revision. It is better, even as a matter of taste and without regard to your wishes which would, of course, be conclusive."[35] When Robert still seemed discontent, Hay again assured him that the ultimate say would be his: "I was very sorry to see by a letter you wrote to Nicolay the other day that you were still not satisfied with my assurance that I would make those first chapters right. Even before you read them I had struck out of my own copy here nearly everything you objected to. . . . Since then I have gone over the whole thing twice again, reading every line so far as possible from your point of view, and I don't think there is a word left in it that would displease you. But of course before final publication I shall give you another hack at it, with plenary blue-pencil powers." Hay told Robert that the biography would be reverential: "Year after year of study has shown me more clearly than ever how infinitely greater your father was than anybody about him, greater than ever we imagined while he lived. There is nothing to explain or apologize for from beginning to end. He is the one unapproachably great figure of a great epoch."[36] (In 1866, Hay had declared that "Lincoln with all his foibles, is the greatest character since Christ.")[37]

In the absence of the full manuscript, it is impossible to determine how much more blue-penciling Robert engaged in. There may have been precious little; Hay's 470 handwritten pages on Lincoln and the Army of the Potomac, now in the Library of Congress, bear no signs of Robert's censorship, nor do the two dozen chapters in the Hay Papers at Brown University.[38]

David C. Mearns, a most thoughtful commentator on Robert Todd Lincoln's role in shaping Nicolay and Hay's work, noted that Robert's "devotion to his father's memory was excessive. It was this extravagance which made him more inclined to idolaters than to realists." To a critic who suggested that Robert had "thwarted" history by heavily censoring Nicolay and Hay, Mearns replied, "Taste (not censorship, not thwarting) was always the most powerful influence over Colonel Hay." Robert, he shrewdly observed,

> was throttled with more inhibitions, more inferiorities, than any other well-placed gentleman since the notorious Prince of Denmark. Still, he made a competent Secretary of War, and a charming ambassador to Victoria. He succeeded in business. He was a bit of a snob, perhaps, but he was not ignoble. A possible key to his character could be found in two of his relationships: he treated John Hay as an equal and John Nicolay as his father's hired man. He drew fine but insistent distinctions between public and private life: his mother was his own affair. He was not bent upon thwarting history but upon discharging the responsibilities of the heir of the Lincoln tradition. He considered it his duty to see that his father's place in history was irreproachable, unapproachable even unworldly. To that end, he surrendered himself to the mores of his time. He was, in other words, preponderantly his mother's son.[39]

As Mearns noted, Hay was devoted to good taste; that doubtless led him to engage in self-censorship as he described Lincoln's courtship and marriage. From interviews with Lincoln's friends, most notably Orville H. Browning, Nicolay and Hay had learned much about Lincoln's relations with Mary Todd. Browning revealed that Lincoln had in 1841 broken his engagement to Miss Todd because he had fallen deeply in love with the eighteen-year-old beauty, Matilda Edwards, who did not reciprocate his feelings. Browning added that Lincoln's subsequent bout of intense depression was caused by his conflicted feelings: "Mr. Lincoln became very much attached to her (Miss Matilda Edwards) and finally fell desperately in love with her, and proposed to her, but she rejected him. . . . I think that Mr. Lincoln's aberration of mind resulted entirely from the situation he thus got himself into—he was engaged to Miss Todd, and in love with Miss Edwards, and his conscience troubled him dreadfully for the supposed injustice he had done, and the supposed violation of his word which he had committed."[40]

Apparently without any prompting from Robert, Hay discretely drew a veil over this chapter in Lincoln's intimate life: "It is as useless as it would be indelicate to seek to penetrate in detail the incidents and special causes which produced in his mind this darkness as of the valley of the shadow of death. There was probably nothing worth recording in them; we are only concerned with their effect upon a character which was to be hereafter for all time one of the possessions of the nation. It is enough for us to know that a great trouble came upon him, and that he bore it nobly after his kind."[41]

Browning also revealed that Mary Todd Lincoln's conduct as first lady had grieved her husband: "He has several times told me there [at the White House] that he was constantly under great apprehension lest his wife should do something which would bring him into disgrace."[42] Browning knew how Mary Lincoln had padded expense accounts and payrolls, accepted bribes and kickbacks, and engaged in other unethical practices.[43] Nicolay and Hay were also aware from firsthand experience how Mrs. Lincoln had illegally attached the wages of White House servants and tried to pilfer money from the White House stationery and manure funds.[44] This information they voluntarily suppressed, to avoid offending not only Robert but also their readers' Victorian sense of propriety (which they of course shared). Doubtless for similar reasons, they did not recount the story of Mary Lincoln's tantrums and jealous fits that Adam Badeau had publicly described in 1887.[45]

Nicolay and Hay also hesitated to offend other people, such as the daughter of Lincoln's exasperating secretary of the treasury, Salmon P. Chase. "There is enough in Chase's letters abusing Lincoln behind his back for a quiet scorcher," Hay told Nicolay, "but think of Mrs. Hoyt, if you please."[46] Mrs. Hoyt was Janet (Nettie) Ralston Chase, who lived until 1925.

Contemporaries rightly objected that *Abraham Lincoln: A History* lacked a vivid description of Lincoln's personality and intimate life. As their editor, Richard Watson Gilder, told them, "There is some disappointment that Lincoln himself does not shine on every page of the History." Gilder himself did not object, for he knew "that the History is, in original material as well as in scope, just what we bargained for, and what I knew it was before its publication began. It has, moreover, been a great magazine success. It has both developed and proved an appetite on the part of the public for Lincoln pure and simple that we are extremely desirous to gratify." Gilder wanted Nicolay and Hay to produce a volume entitled "The Personal Traits of Lincoln," which they planned to write but never did.[47]

If some found fault with Nicolay and Hay's work, many applauded it. William Dean Howells called it "not only . . . the most important work yet accomplished in American history," but also "one of the noblest achievements of literary art."[48] In 1888 Robert Todd Lincoln told Hay, "You & Nicolay must be relieved in putting the finishing touches to your great work and you must be gratified at the reception of so much of it as has been published. Many people speak to me & confirm my own opinion of it as a work in every way excellent—not only sustaining but elevating my father's place in History. I shall never cease to be glad that the places you & Nicolay held near him & in his confidence were filled by you & not by others."[49] The historian James Ford Rhodes told them, "your book will demolish the modern theory that an author cannot write modern history impartially."[50]

Later historians tend to agree with Allan Nevins, who condemned Nicolay and Hay's volumes as "an appalling mixture of history and biography, the history now being completely outdated, and the biography so fulsome in its flattery, so blind to all Lincoln's shortcomings and defects as he grew up into greatness, that it is now almost worthless."[51]

Before the Lincoln papers became available to scholars in 1947, however, Nicolay and Hay's biography was a valuable source book for historians.[52] As William E. Barton put it in 1929, "The limitations of this work are known and lamented by all Lincoln students. . . . But even so, this work is an invaluable storehouse of authentic Lincoln material, prized and utilized by all Lincoln students."[53] But with the opening of the Lincoln papers and the publication of *The Collected Works of Abraham Lincoln* six years later, the Nicolay and Hay biography lost much of its usefulness. Other original materials that they had used, such as Hay's White House diary and Nicolay's memos of presidential conversations, were also published by 1949 (though in editions failing to meet modern editorial standards).

So in the twenty-first century, what can be said of *Abraham Lincoln: A History*? Much of Allan Nevins's criticism is sound. To modern ears the implacably partisan and judgmental tone of Nicolay and Hay is so painfully unhistorical as to be virtually unreadable.[54] Instead of explaining why people behaved the way they did, the authors sit in judgment on that behavior, ladling out praise and blame like the Almighty separating the sheep from the goats on Judgment Day. Their tendency to hero worship is tiresome. As Harry E. Pratt noted, "To the authors, Lincoln's every act was wise and righteous."[55] An example occurs early in the biography when Hay commented on Lincoln's decision to join the Whig rather than the Democratic party:

> It showed some moral courage, and certainly an absence of the shuffling politician's fair-weather policy, that Lincoln, in his obscure and

penniless youth, at the very beginning of his career, when he was not embarrassed by antecedents or family connections, and when, in fact, what little social influence he knew would have led him the other way, chose to oppose a furiously intolerant majority, and to take his stand with the party which was doomed to long-continued defeat in Illinois. The motives which led him to take this decisive course are not difficult to imagine. The better sort of people in Sangamon County were Whigs, though the majority were Democrats, and he preferred through life the better sort to the majority.[56]

This passage illustrates another quality of the biography that grates on modern sensibilities: class snobbishness. After the initial chapters appeared in the *Century*, C. O. Poole observed that Nicolay and Hay were "aiming . . . to make a story popular with the '*classes*' as against the '*masses*.' It will result in delineating the real Lincoln about as well as does a wax figure in the museum."[57] Hay in particular cherished "respectability" and looked contemptuously upon the "vulgar." Anyone who slogs through all ten volumes may eventually sympathize with the journalist and historian David Rankin Barbee, who declared that "Hay was such a damned intellectual snob,—so superior to everybody, including Jehovah, that you want to puke as you read him."[58]

The endless stretches where Lincoln disappears also tax the patience of a modern reader, especially when those chapters of historical background have been superseded by scholars whose research is far more extensive than Nicolay and Hay's. One of the more soporific chapters, "The Ohio Line," begins thus:

The American rebellion cannot be studied without constantly bearing in mind the immense geographical area of the United States. From the Allegheny mountains to the Mississippi River, across a territorial breadth of nine degrees of longitude, runs the Ohio River in a south-westerly course; beginning at Pittsburgh among the western spurs of the Alleghenies and ending at Cairo, where it empties itself into the Mississippi. . . . At Cairo, the thousand miles of navigation of the

Ohio are joined to another thousand miles of navigation southward
to New Orleans, and an additional thousand northward on the Mississippi to St. Paul not to mention the Missouri River and various
other tributaries.[59]

Also tedious are long stretches where Nicolay and Hay quote ex-
tensively from documents, many of which they alone had access to,
including letters to Lincoln and passages from diaries kept by cabinet
members and influential military figures. At times, *Abraham Lincoln:
A History* reads like a massively annotated version of Lincoln's collected
writings; the entire first inaugural is given verbatim. At other times,
the biography resembles a documentary history of the war; eight uninterrupted pages are devoted to reproducing the correspondence of the
governor of South Carolina.[60]

Nicolay and Hay treat Lincoln's early life skimpily. Harry E. Pratt
marveled that "they covered the first forty years of Lincoln's life in 282 of
the 4,709 pages of the work."[61] They did not avail themselves of the best
source of information about those years: the interviews and correspondence sedulously conducted and assembled by William H. Herndon.[62]
Herndon rightly complained, "Some of the finest episodes in L's young
life are omitted or evaded or smothered up in *words*."[63]

Another flaw in the biography is Nicolay and Hay's tendency to re-
write the documents they quote. Passages from Nicolay's interviews and
memoranda of conversations are spruced up when incorporated into the
text. Most important, the Lincoln who emerges from the ten volumes is,
as Nathaniel Wright Stephenson complained, "exasperatingly conven-
tional—always the saint and the hero."[64] Lincoln's humanity disappears
beneath the filiopietistic encomiums heaped upon him. Seldom do we
see him vent his anger, succumb to depression, tell bawdy stories, reject
his father, cruelly ridicule his opponents, toss off a clever pun, suffer
domestic misery in a woe-filled marriage, or scramble for political pre-
ferment. No attempt is made to analyze or illuminate his inner life. [65]

He becomes an insufferably respectable paragon of bourgeois virtues. As Herndon rightly complained, the authors "have suppressed many facts, material facts, of Lincoln's life." Rhetorically Herndon asked, "Do you call this history, do you call it biography? No wonder that L. had a contempt for all history and biography."[66]

Some recent Lincoln authorities are less critical, among them Roy P. Basler, editor of *The Collected Works of Abraham Lincoln*. In 1974, he told a biographer of Hay, "As, I suspect, one of the few people yet alive who once read Nicolay and Hay complete, . . . I think it remains indispensable, especially for the presidency, and will not be superseded." Basler pointed out that the authors "were writing not merely a biography of a public man but a history of the nation in his time." That history, Basler concluded,

> stands up today in my opinion better than any other work so comprehensive, written by any historian contemporary of Nicolay and Hay. Comparing [Carl] Sandburg or [James G.] Randall's work on Lincoln's presidential years with N. & H., I do not find that either made revisions of the essential story told by N. & H., which stand out. They did fill in many niches, of course. On Lincoln's early life both Sandburg and [Albert J.] Beveridge added something, not only to N. & H.'s account but to Herndon's. On the whole, Beveridge, for all of his facade of documentation, was inaccurate to the extent that from the start he let his bias toward S. A. Douglas dictate his selection of fact and opinion. Sandburg erred by dumping everything in uncritically, but he mixed it with a flair that made the blend far truer to Lincoln than Beveridge in my opinion. . . . Nicolay and Hay seem to me to make use of the stuff of history as well as or better than most of their successors, including Bruce Catton. They did not choose, wisely I think, to write an intimate biography, because they were not equipped to do the job. . . . [Sandburg] absorbed it [Nicolay and Hay's biography] and then began stuffing himself with everything else he

could clip out of any source available, to regurgitate like the poetic pigeon he was, something which many have found to be good reading, but Edmund Wilson found "insufferable." Sandburg simply could not have begun without reading Nicolay and Hay.[67]

1

ELECTION DAY 1860 AND CABINET MAKING

$\mathcal{N}$icolay and Hay worked for Lincoln during the presidential campaign of 1860 and were with him on Election Day, November 6. That morning, Springfield shed its customary tranquility as cannons boomed to herald the dawn. Augmenting their din were bands blaring music from wagons drawn about the city to arouse the populace. Men loitering around the polls contributed their mite to the "good-natured clamor." There was little violence, though the editor of the *Illinois State Register* was caned by a gentleman whom he had accused of lying.[1]

At the statehouse, Lincoln, "as unconcerned as the most obscure man in the nation," received visitors as he sat in an armchair that dwarfed him.[2] "Nobody expects to find Mr. Lincoln a portly man, but at first sight his slenderness strikes one as even beyond what had been expected," a journalist noted. Among his callers were "some rough-jacketed constituents who, having voted for him, and expressed a wish to look at their man, came in timidly, were kindly received, and, after a dumb sitting of a quarter of an hour, went away, thoroughly satisfied in every manner." Then came a few New Yorkers, who, Lincoln thought, should have remained home to vote. He told one resident of the Empire State that "he was afraid there were too many of us from New York that day." When that caller asked Lincoln whether the South would secede if the Republicans captured the White House, he "said they might make a little stir about it before [the inauguration], but if they waited until after his inauguration and for some overt act, *they would wait all their lives.*"[3] When queried about rail-splitting, he showed how it had been performed when he was young and contrasted that technique with the one then employed, which he acknowledged was superior. He had intended to vote late in the day to avoid crowds; in midafternoon, however, when informed that there were few people at the polls, he decided to cast his ballot then. The day before, he had been asked for whom he would vote. "Yates," he replied puckishly, referring to Richard Yates, the Republican gubernatorial candidate. When pressed how he would vote for president, he responded, "How vote? Well, undoubtedly like an Ohio elector of which I will tell you—by ballot."[4]

As he approached the courthouse, accompanied by Ozias M. Hatch and other friends, "the dense crowd immediately began to shout with the wild abandon that characterizes the impulsive heart of the west," Hay reported to the Providence, Rhode Island, *Journal.* "The crowded throng respectfully opened a passage for him from the street to the polls." Nicolay observed his boss approach the courthouse steps "thronged with People, who welcomed him with immense cheering, and followed him in dense numbers along the hall and up stairs into the Court room, which was also crowded. Here the applause became absolutely deafening, and from the time he entered the room and until he cast his vote and again left it, there was wild huzzaing, waving of hats, and all sorts of demonstrations of applause,—rendering all other noise insignificant and futile." A correspondent of the New York *Tribune* noted that all traces of partisanship "seemed to be suddenly abandoned. Even the distributors of the Douglas tickets shouted and swung their hats as wildly as the rest." An elderly gentleman with an armload of Democratic documents led several cheers for him. Before depositing his ballot, Lincoln cut off the names of the presidential electors so that he would not be voting for himself.[5] One wag cried out, "You ought to vote for Douglas, Uncle Abe, he has done all he could for you."[6]

After shaking many hands, Lincoln returned to the statehouse, making his way through a dense crowd of people "seizing his hands, and throwing their arms around his neck, body or legs and grasping his coat or anything they could lay hands on, and yelling and acting like madmen."[7] He spent the rest of the afternoon at the capitol. A St. Louis journalist recalled that he "had a lively interest in the election," but that "he scarcely ever alluded to himself or his candidacy." Rather he "was interested in the fortunes of the local candidates of his town, county and State and to have heard his remarks one would have concluded that the District Attorneyship of a county in Illinois was of far more importance than the Presidency itself." At one point "he mentioned a candidate for the Legislature in one of these counties who he hoped would be elected, and he would be, Mr. Lincoln added, 'if he didn't find Abe Lincoln too heavy a load to carry on the same ticket.'" Later "he said that elections in this country were like 'big boils'—they caused a great deal of pain before they came to a head, but after the trouble was over the body was in better health than before. He hoped that the bitterness of the canvass would pass away 'as easily as the core of a boil.'"

When one of his friends mentioned the New York fusionists—supporters of Lincoln's three opponents who had belatedly agreed on a joint slate of electors—Lincoln "remarked that they would probably get into such a row going up Salt River as to 'obstruct navigation' thereafter." To Ozias Hatch's observation "that it was lucky for him that women couldn't vote, otherwise the monstrous portraits of him which had been circulated during the canvass by friends would surely defeat him," Lincoln replied smilingly, "Hatch, I tell you there is a great deal more in that idea than you suppose," and "then related a story of a Presbyterian church in McLean County in Illinois holding a congregational meeting to vote a call to a pastor. The elders and deacons and principal men in the church had united in recommending a certain man, and it was supposed he would be called unanimously; but in an evil hour somebody got hold of the man's likeness and exhibited it to the sisters. They didn't like the wart he had on his nose, so they turned out in force and voted down the call."

When a dispatch arrived from Charleston, South Carolina, expressing the wish that Lincoln would win because, if he did, the Palmetto State "would soon be free," Lincoln laughed "because the sentiment seemed a familiar one inasmuch as . . . he had received several letters, some signed by the writers, and some anonymous, of the same tenor and effect." He handed the message to Hatch, telling him "that the sender of it would bear watching."[8]

About 7 P.M., the crowd at the statehouse flooded into the room where Lincoln awaited the returns. When someone suggested that they be cleared out, he immediately objected, saying "he had never done such a thing in his life and wouldn't commence now." Soon the room was jammed. The candidate remained as "calm and collected as ever in his life but there was a nervous twitch on his countenance when the messenger from the telegraphic office entered, that indicated an anxiety within that no coolness from without could repress." When the first dispatch arrived from Decatur, showing a significant Republican gain over the previous election, it was greeted with shouts and taken from the governor's office to the assembly chamber "as a trophy to be read to the crowd." At 8 P.M. a dispatch from Jacksonville indicating a 210-vote Republican gain "seemed to gratify Mr. Lincoln exceedingly."[9]

An hour later, Lincoln and some friends left the statehouse for the telegraph office to await the returns. As fragmentary reports came in from nearby counties, "Lincoln seemed to understand their bearing on the general result in the State and commented upon every return by way of comparison with previous elections. He understood at a glance whether it was a loss or a gain to his party." He was gleeful when news arrived from Saline County, where in 1856 the Republican presidential candidate had received one lone vote while Democrat James Buchanan got nearly 2,000; but now three of the main precincts in that southern Illinois county gave Lincoln a majority of nearly 200 over Stephen A. Douglas.

"He laughed heartily and exclaimed that that was 'a tribute from Egypt to the success of our public school fund.'" As the good news rolled in, Lincoln's friends and the telegraph operators could hardly contain their enthusiasm. The nominee himself, however, remained calm. The New York *Tribune* reporter noted that he "accepted everything with an almost immovable tranquility." He did not seek "to conceal in the slightest degree the keen interest he felt in every new development; but, while he seemed to absorb it all with great satisfaction, the intelligence moved him to less energetic display of gratification than the others indulged in. He appeared, indeed, to be as fully alive to the smaller interest of some local districts, in which the fortunes of his friends were concerned, as to the wider and more universally important regions."[10]

A dispatch announcing that Lincoln had won by 2,500 votes in Chicago occasioned a "joyous thrill." The candidate instructed, "Send it to the boys" in the statehouse. There "*Old* men, young, middle aged, clergymen and *all*" responded by "*singing, yelling! shouting, . . . [and] dancing.*"[11] Lincoln was equally delighted with good news from St. Louis, where he bested Douglas by over 900 votes. When word from Pittsburgh arrived indicating that Lincoln carried Allegheny County by 10,000 votes, he "remarked that this was better than expected."[12]

Soon returns trickled in from more distant points. Lincoln betrayed some anxiety about the result in New York, "remarking that 'the news would come quick enough if it was good, and if bad, he was not in any hurry to hear it.'" Around 10:30, in response to a hopeful message from Thurlow Weed, Lincoln "remarked that the news was satisfactory so far, only it was not conclusive." Then New Jersey returns "began to excite surprise, as report after report gave Fusion [i.e., Douglas-Bell-Breckinridge] majorities." Offsetting this bad news were "cheering returns from New England, which by this time, past eleven o'clock, began to arrive in profusion." They "banished the depressing effect of the New Jersey returns." When word came in that Massachusetts had gone for him by 50,000, Lincoln called it "a clear case of the Dutch taking Holland."[13]

As expected, Lincoln carried Pennsylvania easily, a result that he said could be accounted for "only on one supposition and that is that the Quakers voted."[14] (The Democrats had feared a large Quaker turnout in Philadelphia, a city that Lincoln won with 52 percent of the vote.)[15] Worries about New York, however, persisted.

After hours of mostly positive news, returns began arriving from Democratic states. "Now we should get a few licks back," Lincoln remarked.[16] As predicable results continued to roll in from the South, Lincoln and his friends took a break shortly after midnight, visiting the collation prepared by the women of Springfield, who "surrounded, and took possession of, and clung to" the candidate. "The female enthusiasm bubbled up so spontaneously that somehow . . . a movement began to kiss the 'dear man.' Before he had time to either protest or retreat at least a half dozen girls and their mothers had saluted him with hearty kisses on the cheek." Lincoln's "good-humored resistance was quite in vain as he finally yielded with the suggestion that this was 'a form of coercion not prohibited by the Constitution or Congress.' He surrendered meekly enough and took the proffered kisses as one of the duties which he had, on that day, been elected. The women simplified his task by forming a line in single file and circling around the table as they greeted him with their salutes on the 'fire and fall back' principle." He had come "as near being killed by kindness as a man can conveniently be without serious results." After partaking of the "oceans of coffee and continents of food," he and his companions returned to the telegraph office. There encouraging news from New York thrilled Lincoln's companions, but he observed solemnly, "Not too fast, my friends. Not too fast, it may not be over yet."

When even more favorable reports arrived, Jesse K. Dubois asked, "Well, Uncle Abe, are you satisfied now?" Lincoln "replied with a smile, 'Well, the agony is most over, and you will soon be able to go to bed.'" Upon learning that John Bell, the nominee of the Constitutional Union party, had carried Virginia, Lincoln "suggested that this was the most hopeful return for the peace of the country he had heard and he hoped the majority was so large as to crush out the fire-eaters completely. He spoke with considerable emphasis and satisfaction about the strength shown for the conservative American [i.e., Constitutional Union party] ticket in the border States."

Finally, when definitive word of his victory in New York reached Springfield, he read the fateful dispatch "with evident marks of pleasure."[17] So did the crowd at the statehouse, where men "pushed each other—threw up their hats—hurrahed—cheered for Lincoln—cheered for [Illinois Senator Lyman] Trumbull—cheered for New York—cheered for everybody—and some actually lay down on the carpeted floor and rolled over and over." Men dashed through the streets to inform the citizenry that Lincoln had won. "Springfield went off like one immense cannon report, with shouting from houses, shouting from stores, shouting from house tops, shouting from every-where. Parties ran through the streets singing 'Ain't I glad I've joined the Republicans' till they were too hoarse to speak." Throughout the night "there was howling for Lincoln—cheers for 'Old Abe' kept up, and towards morning some of the boys procured a cannon and fired several rounds."[18]

After accepting hearty congratulations, Lincoln remarked, "I feel a great responsibility. God help me, God help me."[19] As he prepared to leave, a messenger announced that he had won Springfield by 69 votes. This good news prompted him to abandon his reserve and give "a sudden exuberant utterance—neither a cheer nor a crow, but something partaking of the nature of each. And then, laughing contentedly, he said good night to the little company." (Though he won Springfield, he lost Sangamon County by 42 votes.)[20]

While Dubois dashed off to inform the crowd at the capitol, Lincoln returned home.[21] Later, when serenaders called there, Mrs. Lincoln re-portedly "cursed—swore and held him back, so that it was with difficulty that he went out to meet the people."[22]

The following excerpts are from Nicolay and Hay, *Abraham Lincoln: A History*, 10 vols. (New York: Century, 1890), 3:345–47, 372–74:

The work of framing the new Cabinet was mainly performed on the evening of the Presidential election. After the polls were closed on the 6th of November (so Mr. Lincoln related a year or two later), the superintendent of the telegraph at Springfield invited him to his office to remain and read the dispatches as they should come in. He accepted the offer; and reporting himself in due time at the telegraph office, from which all other visitors were excluded at 9 o'clock, awaited the result of the eventful day. Soon the telegrams came thick and fast—first from the neighboring precincts and counties; then from the great Western cities, Chicago, St. Louis, Cincinnati; and finally from the capitals of the doubtful States, Indiana, Ohio, Pennsylvania, and the Empire State of New York. Here in this little room, in the company of two or three silent operators moving about their mysteriously clicking instruments, and recording with imperturbable gravity the swift throbbing messages from near and far, Mr. Lincoln read the reports as they came, first in fragmentary dribblets, and later in the rising and swelling stream of cheering news.

There was never a closer calculator of political probabilities than himself. He was completely at home among election figures. All his political life he had scanned tables of returns with as much care and accuracy as he analyzed and scrutinized maxims of government and platforms of parties. Now, as formerly, he was familiar with all the turning-points in contested counties and "close" districts, and knew by heart the value of each and every local loss or gain and its relation to the grand result. In past years, at the close of many a hot campaign, he had searched out the comfort of victory from a discouraging and adverse-looking column of figures, or correctly read the fatal omen of defeat in some single announcement from a precinct or county.

Silently, as they were transcribed, the operators handed him the messages, which he laid on his knee while he adjusted his

spectacles, and then read and re-read several times with deliberation. He had not long to wait for indications. From a scattering
beginning, made up of encouraging local fragments, the hopeful news rose to almost uninterrupted tidings of victory. Soon
a shower of congratulatory telegrams fell from the wires, and
while his partisans and friends in all parts of the country were
thus shaking hands with him "by lightning" [i.e., via telegraph]
over the result, he could hear the shouts and speeches of his
Springfield followers, gathered in the great hall of the Statehouse across the street.

Of course his first emotions were those of a kindling pleasure and pride at the completeness of his success. But this was
only a momentary glow. He was indeed President-elect; but with
that consciousness there fell upon him the appalling shadow of
his mighty task and responsibility. It seemed as if he suddenly
bore the whole world upon his shoulders, and could not shake it
off; and sitting there in the yet early watches of the night, he read
the still coming telegrams in a sort of absentminded mechanical routine, while his inner man took up the crushing burden
of his country's troubles, and traced out the laborious path of
future duties. "When I finally bade my friends good-night and
left that room," said Lincoln, "I had substantially completed
the framework of my Cabinet as it now exists." . . .

[He chose for Secretary of State, William H. Seward, of
New York; for Secretary of the Treasury, Salmon P. Chase, of
Ohio; for Secretary of War, Simon Cameron, of Pennsylvania;
for Secretary of the Navy, Gideon Welles, of Connecticut; for
Secretary of the Interior, Caleb B. Smith, of Indiana; for At-
torney-General, Edward Bates, of Missouri; for Postmaster-
General, Montgomery Blair, of Maryland.]

The Senate confirmed all these nominations without delay;
and on the day after, March 6, most of the appointees were
formally inducted into office. That evening occurred the first
Cabinet meeting, for introduction and acquaintance; and the
new President greeted his Cabinet at the Executive Mansion
substantially as he had planned it, on the night of the November
election, in the little telegraph office at Springfield.

Carping critics might indeed at the moment have specified defects, incongruities, jealousies, and seeds of possible discord and disaster in the new Cabinet, but we can now understand, that they neither comprehended the man who was to dominate and govern it, nor the storms of state which, as captain and crew, he and they were to encounter and outride. He needed advisers, helpers, executive eyes and hands, not alone in department routine, but in the higher qualities of leadership and influence; above all, his principal motive seems to have been representative character, varied talent—in a word, combination. Statesmanship implies success; success demands cooperation, popular sympathy, and support. He wished to combine the experience of Seward, the integrity of Chase, the popularity of Cameron; to hold the West with Bates, attract New England with Welles; please the Whigs through Smith, and convince the Democrats through Blair.

Mr. Lincoln possessed a quick intuition of human nature and of the strength or weakness of individual character. His whole life had been a practical study of the details and rivalries of local partisanship. He was, moreover, endowed in yet unsuspected measure with a comprehensive grasp of great causes and results in national politics. He had noted and heralded the alarming portent of the slavery struggle. With more precision than any contemporary, he had defined the depth and breadth of the moral issues and rights it involved; he had led the preliminary victory at the November polls. Now that secession was proclaimed in every Cotton State, his simple logic rose above minor considerations to the peril and the protection of the nation, to the assault on and the defense of the Constitution. He saw but the ominous cloud of civil war in front, and the patriotic faith and enthusiasm of the people behind him. The slogan of a Seward committee, a Chase delegation, or a Cameron clan was but the symbol and promise of a Wide-Awake club to vote for freedom, or of an armed regiment on the battlefield to maintain it. Neither did anyone yet suspect his delicate tact in management, strength of will, and firmness of purpose. In weaker hands such a Cabinet would have been a hot-bed of strife; under him it became a tower of strength. He made these selections because he wanted a council of distinctive and diverse, yet able, influential, and representative, men, who should be a harmonious group of constitutional advisers and executive lieutenants—not a board of regents holding the great seal in commission and intriguing for the succession.

2

THE FORT SUMTER CRISIS: MARCH–APRIL 1861

On Lincoln's first day in office, the Fort Sumter crisis unexpectedly demolished his carefully planned strategy for dealing with the seceded states. In his conciliatory inaugural address, he had promised the South not to interfere with slavery where it already existed, not to appoint obnoxious strangers to fill federal offices in the South, and not to try to collect import revenues against the will of the people in the seceded states. At the suggestion of Secretary of State–designate William Henry Seward and of others, he dropped belligerent language threatening forcibly to retake federal forts, arsenals, and other facilities that the Confederates had seized. He hoped the gentle tone of his message as well as the mild policy statements would prevent any sudden outbreak of hostilities; time would work its healing wonders on the hotheads who had precipitated the crisis, the sober second thought would prevail, and the seceded states would recognize the error of their ways and return to the fold. But no sooner had he delivered his address than he received fateful word from Charleston Harbor: the federal garrison was running low on food and would be starved out within a few weeks unless resupplied. But if Lincoln did send fresh supplies, South Carolina forces would probably attack the ships and Fort Sumter as well. If he allowed the fort to be starved into submission, he would tacitly recognize the legitimacy of secession and enrage his Northern constituents.

Nicolay and Hay describe the dilemma succinctly (*Abraham Lincoln: A History*, 3:375–79):

*I*n his letter of January 4, General [Winfield] Scott had promised Mr. Lincoln that from time to time he would keep him informed of the situation of military affairs. This promise the general failed to redeem; probably not through any intentional neglect, but more likely because in the first place [President James] Buchanan's policy of delay, indecision, and informal negotiation with the conspirators left everything in uncertainty; and, secondly, because the attention of the Administration (and measurably of the whole country) was turned to hopes of compromise, especially through the labors of the Peace Convention.

The rebels, on their part, were absorbed in the formation of the provisional government at Montgomery; Lincoln was making his memorable journey from Springfield to Washington by way of the chief cities of the North; the Fort Pickens truce was practically a secret; and thus the military status was for the time being lost sight of beyond the immediate neighborhood of Charleston. Since the reorganization of Buchanan's Cabinet on December 31, and the expulsion or defection of traitors from the departments and from Congress, the whole North had breathed somewhat easier. The firing on the *Star of the West* had created a storm of indignation; but this, too, quickly subsided, and by a sort of common consent all parties and sections looked to the incoming Administration as the only power which could solve the national crisis.

The key-note of such a solution was given in the inaugural of the new President. This announced a decided, though not a violent, change of policy. Buchanan's course had been one professedly of conciliation, but practically of ruinous concession. Lincoln, receiving from his hands the precious trust of the Government,—not in its original integrity, but humbled, impaired, diminished, and threatened,—announced his purpose of conciliation, conservation, and restoration. "The policy chosen," said he, "looked to the exhaustion of all peaceful measures before a resort to any stronger ones. It sought only to hold the public places and property not already wrested from the Government, and to collect the revenue, relying for the rest on time, discussion, and the ballot-box. It promised a continuance of the mails at Government expense to the very people who were resisting the Government, and it gave repeated pledges against any disturbance to any of the people or any of their rights. Of all that which a President might constitutionally and justifiably do in such a case, everything was forborne without which it was believed possible to keep the Government on foot."

This pacific purpose was now, however, destined to receive a rude shock. When on the morning of the 5th of March Lincoln went to his office in the Executive Mansion, he found a letter from Mr. Holt, still acting as Secretary of War, giving him news of vital importance received on the morning of the inauguration—namely, that Fort Sumter must, in the lapse of a few weeks at most, be strongly reenforced or summarily abandoned. Major Anderson had in the previous week made an examination of his provisions. There was bread for twenty-eight days; pork for a somewhat longer time; beans, rice, coffee, and sugar for different periods from eight to forty days.

He had at the same time consulted his officers on the prospects and possibilities of relief and reenforcement. They unanimously reported that before Sumter could be permanently or effectively succored a combined land and naval force must attack and carry the besieging forts and batteries, and hold the secession militia at bay, and that such an undertaking would at once concentrate at Charleston all the volunteers, not alone of South Carolina, but of the adjacent States as well. "I confess," wrote Anderson, transmitting the reports and estimates of his nine officers, "that I would not be willing to risk my reputation on an attempt to throw reenforcements into this harbor within the time for our relief rendered necessary by the limited supply of our provisions, and with a view of holding possession of the same, with a force of less than twenty thousand good and well-disciplined men." Mr. Holt, quoting from previous instructions to and reports from the major, added that this declaration "takes the Department by surprise, as his previous correspondence contained no such intimation."

Retrospective criticism as to why or how such a state of things had been permitted to grow up was, of course, useless. Here was a most portentous complication, not of Lincoln's own creating, but which he must nevertheless meet and overcome. He had counted on the soothing aid of time; time, on the contrary, was in this emergency working in the interest of rebellion. General Scott was at once called into council, but his sagacity and experience could afford neither suggestion nor encouragement. That same night he returned the papers to the President with a somewhat lengthy indorsement reciting the several events which led to, and his own personal efforts to avert, this contingency, but ending with the gloomy conclusion: "Evacuation seems almost inevitable, and in this view our distinguished Chief Engineer (Brigadier Totten) concurs—if indeed the worn-out garrison be not assaulted and carried in the present week." This was a disheartening, almost a disastrous, beginning for the Administration. The Cabinet had only that day been appointed and confirmed. The Presidential advisers had not yet taken their posts, all had not even signified their acceptance. There was an impatient multitude clamoring for audience, and behind these swarmed an army of office-seekers. Everything was urgency and confusion, everywhere was ignorance of method and routine. Rancor and hatred filled the breasts of political opponents departing from power; suspicion and rivalry possessed partisan adherents seeking advantage and promotion. As yet, Lincoln virtually stood alone, face to face with the appalling problems of the present and the threatening responsibilities of the future. Doubtless in this juncture he remembered and acted upon a biblical precedent which in after days of trouble and despondency he was wont to quote for justification or consolation. When the children of Israel murmured on the shore of the Red Sea, Moses told them to "stand still and see the salvation of the Lord." Here, at the very threshold of his Presidential career, Lincoln had need to practice the virtue of patience—one of the cardinal elements of his character, acquired in many a personal and political tribulation.

3

DISTRIBUTING PATRONAGE: 1861

$\mathcal{O}$n April 6, Lincoln made the fateful decision to order the fleet that had been assembled at New York to resupply Fort Sumter. While awaiting word from Charleston, he resumed the onerous chore of distributing patronage to worthy Republicans and removing pro-secession office-holders. By the mid-nineteenth century, a spoils system had become well established, and civil servants were appointed not on the basis of merit but political influence. Congressmen, senators, governors, cabinet members, and local political bosses had a say in the distribution of offices.[1]

The press complained about Lincoln's absorption in patronage matters. "Mr. Lincoln suffered his time to be occupied, his mind agitated, and his feelings harrassed [*sic*] by office-seekers, to an extent never before known, perhaps, in the history of our Government," editorialized the Cincinnati *Gazette*.[2] Another paper in the Queen City indignantly observed that the president's "time is precious to the country. The honor and material interests of the nation demand of him the clear-headed consideration of the most delicate and difficult problems ever before a president, but he is remorselessly victimized by the party vampires, and the time and attention that belongs to the country are occupied in squabbles between office hunters who are in person and politics utterly contemptible."[3] In April, *Frank Leslie's Illustrated Newspaper* lamented that a "precious month has been lost in the weighing whether Hiram Barney or Simeon Draper shall have this or that position."[4] John W.

Forney of the Philadelphia *Press* likened the president to a housewife who early one morning was sweeping the kitchen as her children slept upstairs. Suddenly the house caught fire. "The industrious mother, however, determined to *finish her sweeping*; and so lost her house and her children with it." Lincoln agreed with that point, telling one office seeker, "I must not be worried by those who desire to furnish one end of our National Government while the Southern portion of it is wrapped in flames."[5] Another Philadelphia journalist, James E. Harvey, complained that while "the Government is crumbling under our feet, the only question considered is whether one man or another shall be a tide waiter, a village Postmaster or an Indian agent."[6] The Indianapolis *Journal* scolded Lincoln for letting "politicians use up his time with personal solicitations, when he should have kicked the first man who approached him about an appointment not actually needed in the prosecution of the public business out of his sight."[7] The Washington correspondent of the Charleston *Mercury* sneered that "grave affairs of State are to him of little moment in comparison with the distribution of rewards amongst those who have served him faithfully."[8] Another Democratic paper thought the administration's motto could be summarized thus: "The spoils first, the country last."[9]

Lincoln rose early and spent at least twelve hours a day meeting with callers.[10] He was "profoundly disgusted with the importunate herd of office beggars" and complained about being cooped up all day dealing with them. A journalist feared that such "confinement will ruin him if continued."[11] On March 13, he reportedly had to cut short his office hours in order to take a nap.[12] Five days later, it was reported that Lincoln's time "is almost wholly engrossed in hearing applications for office. His order is, that all visitors shall be treated courteously and have a fair opportunity of communicating with him personally." Such a schedule "exposes him to harassing importunity, and seriously interferes with his own comfort and health. It has now become so vexatious that his best friends think some decided corrective should be applied."[13]

One corrective was to have each caller screened by the sober, dignified Nicolay, who "was decidedly German in his manner of telling men what he thought of them."[14] The young secretary was unflatteringly described as "the bulldog in the ante-room" with a disposition "sour and crusty"; as "very disagreeable and uncivil"; and as "a grim Cerebrus of Teutonic descent" who "has a very unhappy time of it answering the impatient demands of the gathering, growing crowd of applicants which obstructs passage, hall and ante-room."[15] A more charitable portrait was drawn by the journalist John Russell Young, who said Nicolay "had the close, methodical, silent German way about him. Scrupulous, polite, calm, obliging, with the gift of hearing other people talk; coming and going about the Capitol like a shadow; with the soft, sad smile that seemed to come only from the eyes; prompt as lightning to take a hint or an idea; one upon whom a suggestion was never lost, and if it meant a personal service, sure of the prompt spontaneous return." All in all, Nicolay was a "man without excitements or emotions, . . . absorbed in the President, and seeing that the Executive business was well done."[16] One of his assistants, William O. Stoddard, called Nicolay a "fair French and German scholar, with some ability as a writer and much natural acuteness, he nevertheless—thanks to a dyspeptic tendency—had developed an artificial manner the reverse of 'popular,' and could say 'no' about as disagreeably as any man I ever knew." But, Stoddard pointed out, Nicolay served the president well; his "chief qualification for the very important post he occupied, was his devotion to the President and his incorruptible honesty Lincoln-ward." The youthful German "measured all things and all men by their relations to the President, and was of incalculable service in fending off much that would have been unnecessary labor and exhaustion to his overworked patron." Stoddard thought that Lincoln "showed his good judgment of men when he put Mr. Nicolay where he is, with a kind and amount of authority which it is not easy to describe."[17]

Nicolay's principal assistant, John Hay, also helped breast the surging tide, a task that he found disagreeable. The relations between Hay and Lincoln were like those between Alexander Hamilton and George Washington when the former served as the latter's principal aide. John Russell Young recalled that Hay "knew the social graces and amenities, and did much to make the atmosphere of the war[-]environed White House grateful, tempering unreasonable aspirations, giving to disappointed ambitions the soft answer which turneth away wrath, showing, as Hamilton did in similar offices, the tact and common sense which were to serve him as they served Hamilton in wider spheres of public duty." (Hay's tactfulness was put to the test one day by a gentleman who insisted that he must see Lincoln immediately. "The President is engaged now," replied Hay. "What is your mission?" "Do you know who I am?" asked the caller. "No, I must confess I do not," said Hay. "I am the son of God," came the answer. "The President will be delighted to see you when you come again. And perhaps you will bring along a letter of introduction from your father," retorted the quick-witted secretary.)[18] Young, who often visited the White House during the Civil War, called Hay "brilliant" and "chivalrous," quite "independent, with opinions on most questions," which he expressed freely. At times sociable, Hay could also be "reserved" and aloof, "with just a shade of pride that did not make acquaintanceship spontaneous." Hay, Young said, combined "the genius for romance and politics as no one . . . since Disraeli," and judged that he was well "suited for his place in the President's family." Young depicted Hay as "a comely young man with [a] peach-blossom face," "exceedingly handsome—a slight, graceful, boyish figure—'girl in boy's clothes,' as I heard in a sniff from some angry politician." This "young, almost beardless, and almost boyish countenance did not seem to match with official responsibilities and the tumult of action in time of pressure, but he did what he had to do, was always graceful, composed, polite, and equal to the complexities of any situation which might arise." Hay's "old-fashioned speech" was "smooth, low-toned, quick in comprehension, sententious, reserved." People were "not quite sure whether it was the reserve of diffidence or aristocracy," Young remembered. The "high-bred, courteous" Hay was "not one with whom the breezy overflowing politician would be apt to take liberties." Young noticed "a touch of sadness in his temperament" and concluded that Hay "had the personal attractiveness as well as the youth of Byron" and "was what Byron might have been if grounded on good principles and with the wholesome discipline of home."[19]

Others added touches to Young's portrait. One of his professors at Brown University recalled that Hay "was modest even to diffidence, often blushing to the roots of his hair when he rose to recite."[20] A college friend recalled that Hay's "quick perception, ready grasp of an idea and wonderfully retentive memory, made a mere pastime of study. His enthusiasm was boundless, and his love for and appreciation of the beautiful in nature and in art was acutely developed. If he was smitten with the charms of a pretty girl, he raved and walked the room pouring out his sentiment in a flood of furious eloquence. He would apostrophize a beautiful sunset till the last glow had expired."[21] Hay's roommate at Brown, William Leete Stone, said he was "of a singularly modest and retiring disposition," yet with "so winning a manner that no one could be in his presence, even for a few moments, without falling under the spell which his conversation and companionship invariably cast upon all who came within his influence."[22]

Of that conversation, Joseph Bucklin Bishop observed,

> He loved to talk, and his keen joy in it was so genuine and so obvious that it infected his listeners. He was as good a listener as he was a talker, never monopolizing the conversation. . . . He talked without the slightest sign of effort or premeditation, said his good things as if he owed their inspiration to the listener, and never exhibited a shadow of consciousness of his own brilliancy. His manner toward the conversation of others was the most winning form of compliment conceivable. Every person who spent a half-hour or more with him was sure to go away, not only charmed with Hay, but uncommonly well pleased with himself.[23]

Clark E. Carr described Hay as a "bright, rosy-faced, boyish-looking young man." Carr had never met "a young man or boy who charmed me as he did when he looked at me with his mischievous hazel eyes from under a wealth of dark brown hair. He was, for those days, elegantly dressed,—better than any of us; so neatly, indeed, that he would . . . have been set down as a 'dude' at sight."[24] Logan Hay remarked that his cousin John was "a different type from the rest of the Hay family. He had a magnetic personality—more culture."[25] A newspaperman who saw Hay in 1861 recalled that he was "a young, good-looking fellow, well, almost foppishly dressed, with by no means a low down opinion of himself, either physically or mentally, with plenty of self-confidence for anybody's use, a brain active and intellectual, with a full budget of small talk for the ladies or anybody else, and both eyes keeping a steady lookout for the interests of 'number one.'"[26] In early 1861, Frederick Augustus Mitchel, who attended Brown when Hay was a student there, encountered Hay at Willard's Hotel, casually leaning against a cigar stand; in response to Mitchel's congratulations on being named assistant presidential secretary, Hay replied, "Yes. I'm Keeper of the President's Conscience."[27]

Hay was not so much the conscience of the president as he was his surrogate son, far more like Lincoln in temperament and interests than Robert Todd Lincoln. Hay's humor, intelligence, love of word play, fondness for literature, and devotion to his boss made him a source of comfort to the beleaguered president in the loneliness of the White House. Though nineteen years younger than Lincoln, Hay became as much a friend and confidant to the president as the age difference would allow.[28] He frequently wrote letters for Lincoln's signature; most of them were routine, but one—the famous 1864 letter of condolence to the widow Bixby—achieved world renown.[29]

In 1881, when president-elect James A. Garfield invited Hay to serve another term as a White House secretary, he declined, explaining that "contact with the greed and selfishness of office-seekers and the bull-dozing Congressmen is unspeakably repulsive. The constant contact with envy, meanness, ignorance and the swinish selfishness which ignorance breeds needs a stronger heart and a more obedient nervous system than I can boast."[30]

Much as Hay disliked the bull-dozing lawmakers, he felt some compassion for them. On March 6, 1861, he reported that congressmen "are waylaid, dogged, importuned, buttonholed, coaxed and threatened persistently, systematically, and without mercy, by day and by night."[31] An office seeker thought that beleaguered senators and representatives "need almost as much pity" as the president and his cabinet.[32] "I wish there was an office for every deserving working Republican who desired it," wrote an Indiana Congressman a month after the election, "but alas! there will not be one for every fifty, I fear."[33]

In late March, Nicolay persuaded his boss to limit business hours from 10 A.M. to 3 P.M.; soon thereafter he shortened them by two hours and eliminated Saturday visits.[34] According to Hay, Lincoln "pretended to begin business at ten o[']clock in the morning, but in reality the anterooms and halls were full before that hour—people anxious to get the first axe ground. He was extremely unmethodical: it was a four-years struggle on Nicolay's part and mine to get him to adopt some systematic rules. He would break through every regulation as fast as it was made. Anything that kept the people themselves away from him he disapproved—although they nearly annoyed the life out of him by unreasonable complaints & requests."[35]

Readers of the Cincinnati *Gazette* learned that the "President is about the busiest person in Washington. He is working early and late. His time is taken up mostly with the ceaseless tide of office seekers constantly pouring in upon him. . . . His family only see him at dinner, he being compelled from fatigue to retire to his room as soon as he leaves his office." He "is besieged from morning till night in his ante-rooms, in his parlors, in his library, in his office, at his *matins*, at his breakfast, before and after dinner, and *all night*, until wearied and worn he goes to rest."[36] He allowed "himself hardly time to eat—leaving the table always before others."[37] In mid-March, he "looked very bad" and "very much careworn," for he was "overworking himself" as he struggled with patronage matters and the Fort Sumter question.[38] A frustrated office seeker noted that the president "is working himself down to a shadow in the vain struggle to consider every case himself."[39] On March 13, he reportedly "was obliged to deny himself visitors after two o'clock in the afternoon and go to bed."[40] A brief respite in mid-March, when many office seekers abandoned their quest, afforded little relief, for as Lincoln noted, "when the flies commence leaving in the fall, the few remaining ones always begin to bite like the devil."[41]

On March 24, it was reported that the "incessant calls upon the President are terrible. He is disturbed early in the morning and late in the night, and nothing but the persistent efforts of his friends induced him yesterday to issue an order to the effect that he would receive no visits, either of friendship or official, and yet he was intruded upon by some who ought to have commiserated his trouble."[42] By April, according to Edwin M. Stanton, the president was "said to be very much broken down with the pressure in respect to appointments."[43] On April 3, he "became so severely indisposed as to necessitate the exclusion of all visitors."[44] The following day, the New York *Times* declared, "Mr. Lincoln owes a higher duty to the country, to the world, to his own fame, than to fritter away the priceless opportunities of the Presidency in listening to the appeals of competing office-hunters, in whose eyes the loss of a thousand-dollar clerkship would be a catastrophe little inferior to the downfall of the Republic!"[45] Four years later, he asked a Senator, "Can't you and others start a public sentiment in favor of making no changes in offices except for good and sufficient cause? It seems as if the bare thought of going through again what I did the first year here, would crush me."[46]

At first Lincoln planned to examine applications closely to make sure that patient merit was not eclipsed by the unworthy. He told Carl

Schurz in July 1860, "Men like you, who have real merit and do the work, are always too proud to ask for anything; those who do nothing are always the most clamorous for office, and very often get it, because it is the only way to get rid of them. But if I am elected, they will find a tough customer to deal with, and you may depend upon it that I shall know how to distinguish deserving men from the drones."[47]

Lincoln intended to call on his cabinet and Congress to help select applicants, but, as he told his old friend Robert L. Wilson, he "found to his Surprise, that members of his Cabinet, who were equally interested with himself, in the success of his administration, had been recommending parties to be appointed to responsible positions who were often physically, morally, and intellectually unfit for the place." Apparently, he added, "most of the Cabinet officers and members of Congress, had a list of appointments to be made, and many of them were such as ought not to be made, and they knew, and their importunities were urgent in proportion to the unfitness for the appointee." Lincoln said that he "was so badgered with applications for appointments that he thought sometimes that the only way that he could escape from them would be to take a rope and hang himself on one of the trees in the lawn south of the Presidents House."[48] One journalist argued that the president's reluctance to turn over patronage matters to the Cabinet exclusively was wise. Lincoln's "strong desire to see justice done to all the applicants for office" prompted him "to devote his time from early morning to the hours of darkness in examining their papers." The department heads "might favor their peculiar friends . . . but he represents the nation, and endeavors to be impartial."[49]

Congressmen, senators, and cabinet members were less deeply concerned with the success of the administration than with their own short-term political gain. Adam Gurowski, an irascible, combative Polish nobleman and radical abolitionist, noted in his diary that cabinet secretaries "have old party debts to pay, old sores to avenge or to heal, and all this by distributing offices." Through the use of patronage, "everybody is to serve his friends and his party, and to secure his political position. Some of the party leaders seem to me similar to children enjoying a long-expected and ardently wished-for toy. . . . They, the leaders, look to create engines for their own political security."[50] Gurowski was right. Patronage greased the wheels of political machines; party service counted for more than honesty and competence when government jobs were being distributed. Friendship or family ties with the powerful also weighed heavily in the balance. Charles Francis Adams thought that Lincoln, whom he called "a vulgar man, unfitted both by education and nature for the post of President," had "made very bad selections for all branches of the service."[51]

In fact, Lincoln knowingly appointed some questionable men to office. According to Horace White, he enjoyed a reputation in Illinois as "an adept at log-rolling or any political game that did not involve falsity." White, who was secretary of the Republican State Committee of Illinois in the late 1850s, recalled that Lincoln often attended the meetings of that body:

> His judgment was very much deferred to in such matters. He was one of the shrewdest politicians of the State. Nobody had more experience in that way, nobody knew better than he what was passing in the minds of the people. Nobody knew better how to turn things to advantage politically, and nobody was readier to take such advantage, provided it did not involve dishonorable means. He could not cheat people out of their votes any more than out of their money. . . . Mr. Lincoln never gave his assent, so far as my knowledge goes, to any plan or project for getting votes that would not have borne the full light of day. At the same time, he had no objection to the getting of votes by the pledge of offices, nor was he too particular what kind of man got the offices.[52]

Benjamin Moran, longtime secretary of the U. S. legation in London, thought that "Mr. Lincoln's Consular appointments are the very worst yet made in my time."[53]

Lincoln devoted much time to patronage because he wished to unite his party and, by extension, the entire North. As Secretary of the Navy Gideon Welles recalled, Lincoln, while "striving to reconcile and bring into united action opposing views," was "accused of wasting his time in a great emergency on mere party appointments." Welles conceded that "some things were doubtless done, which, under other circumstances and left to himself he would have ordered differently." But, the navy secretary pointed out, extensive "removals and appointments were not only expected, but absolutely necessary, yet never under any administration were greater care and deliberation required."[54] Judicious distribution of offices could help cement the many factions of the Republican organization (former Whigs, Free Soilers, Know Nothings, and anti-Nebraska Democrats) into a harmonious whole.[55]

Nicolay and Hay described vividly the surging tide of office seekers flooding the White House (*Abraham Lincoln: A History*, 4:68–71):

The Sumter fleet finally at sea, the official note sent to [South Carolina] Governor [Francis] Pickens, and the work of enrolling militia for the defense of Washington progressing so satisfactorily, Lincoln again set himself, during the brief respite, to the work of making the new appointments. Ordinarily this is only an act of official favor or partisan reward, which may be performed at leisure; but then it was a work of pressing need, because of the imperative duty of substituting faithful and loyal agents for indifferent or treasonable ones in the public service. That such abounded, the numerous resignations and still more plentiful avowals made manifest beyond a doubt.

The city was full of strangers; the White House full of applicants from the North. At any hour of the day one might see at the outer door and on the staircase, one line going, one coming. In the anteroom and in the broad corridor adjoining the President's office there was a restless and persistent crowd,—ten, twenty, sometimes fifty, varying with the day and hour,—each one in pursuit of one of the many crumbs of official patronage.

They walked the floor; they talked in groups; they scowled at every arrival and blessed every departure; they wrangled with the door-keepers for the right of entrance; they intrigued with them for surreptitious chances; they crowded forward to get even as much as an instant's glance through the half-opened door into the Executive chamber. They besieged the Representatives and Senators who had privilege of precedence; they glared with envy at the Cabinet Ministers who, by right and usage, pushed through the throng and walked unquestioned through the doors. At that day the arrangement of the rooms compelled the President to pass through this corridor and the midst of this throng when he went to his meals at the other end of the Executive Mansion; and thus, once or twice a day, the waiting expectants would be rewarded by the chance of speaking a word, or handing a paper direct to the President himself, a chance which the more bold and persistent were not slow to improve.

At first, Lincoln bore it all with an admirable fortitude acquired in Western political campaigns. But two weeks of this experience on the trip from Springfield to Washington, and six weeks more of such beleaguering in the Executive office, began to tell on his nerves. What with the Sumter discussion, the rebel negotiation, the diplomatic correspondence, he was subjected to a mental strain and irritation that made him feel like a prisoner behind the Executive doors, and the audible and unending tramp of the applicants outside impressed him like an army of jailers. He said he felt like a man letting lodgings at one end of his house, while the other end was on fire. We can well imagine how it intensified the suspense with which he awaited the news from the fleet and the answer to his official communication to the Governor of South Carolina.

Amid such surroundings and labors the President received the news which now reached the whole country from Sumter. It came very gradually—first the military scurry about Charleston; then [Confederate General P. G. T.] Beauregard's demand for a surrender, followed by [Major Robert] Anderson's prompt refusal; and finally, on the morning of Saturday, April 13, the newspapers of Washington, like those of every other city in the Union, North and South, were filled with the startling head-lines and thrilling details of the beginning and progress of an actual bombardment.

That day there was little change in the business routine of the Executive office. Mr. Lincoln was never liable to sudden ex-citement or sudden activity. Through all his life, and through all the unexpected and stirring events of the rebellion, his personal manner was one of steadiness of word and act. It was this quality which, in the earlier stages of the war, conveyed to many of his visitors the false impression of his indifference. His sagacity gave him a marked advantage over other men in enabling him to fore-cast probable events; and when they took place, his great caution restrained his comments and controlled his outward bearing. Oftentimes, when men came to him in the rage and transport of a first indignation over some untoward incident, they were surprised to find him quiet, even serene,—perhaps with a smile on his face and a jest on his lips,—engaged in routine work, and prone to talk of other and more commonplace matters. Of all things the exhibition of mock-heroism was foreign to his nature. Generally it happened that when others in this mood sought him, his own spirit had already been through the fiery trial of resentment—but giving no outward sign, except at times with lowered eyebrow, a slight nodding and shaking of the head, a muttering motion or hard compression of the lips, and, rarely, an emphatic downward gesture with the clenched right hand. His judgment, like his perception, far outran the average mind. While others fumed and fretted at things that were, all his in-ner consciousness was abroad in the wide realm of possibilities, busily searching out the dim and difficult path towards things to be. His easy and natural attention to ordinary occupations afforded no indication of the double mental process which was habitual with him.

So, while the Sumter telegrams were on every tongue and revengeful indignation was in every heart, there was little varia-tion in the business of the Executive Mansion on that eventful Saturday. The miscellaneous gathering was larger there, as it was larger at the Departments, the newspaper and telegraph offices, and the hotels. More leading men and officials called to learn or to impart news. The Cabinet, as by a common impulse, came together and deliberated. All talk, however, was brief, sententious, informal. The issue had not yet been reached. Sumter was still under fire. Nevertheless, the main question required no discussion, not even decision, scarcely an announcement. Jefferson Davis's order and Beauregard's guns had sufficiently defined the coming action of the Government. After this functionaries and people had but a single purpose, a single duty. Lincoln said but little beyond making inquiries about the current reports and criticizing the probability or accuracy of their details, and went on as usual—receiving visitors, listening to suggestions, and signing routine papers throughout the day.

4

FRONTIER GUARDS AT THE WHITE HOUSE:
APRIL 1861

On April 12, war broke out when South Carolina forces bombarded Fort Sumter even before the Union fleet arrived at Charleston. In the midst of the attendant uncertainty in Washington, General Winfield Scott drew up emergency plans in case the capital were attacked. He designated the huge Treasury Building as a refuge for the president and his cabinet, who would take shelter in the basement while troops massed at Lafayette Square.[1] In the meantime, General Scott assigned Major David Hunter to protect the White House. Hunter called on two Republican leaders, Cassius M. Clay of Kentucky and Jim Lane of Kansas, to organize informal units.[2] Clay, who had arrived in Washington on April 15, was preparing to leave for Russia to take up his duties as America's minister to the czar's government. Hastily he assembled the "Clay Battalion," a ragtag company of a few dozen senators, congressmen, clerks, mechanics, and salesmen.[3] The vain, melodramatic Clay appeared at the Executive Mansion "with a sublimely unconscious air, three pistols and an Arkansas toothpick [Bowie knife] and looked like an admirable vignette to 25-cents-worth of yellow-covered romance," according to Hay.[4] Supplementing these men were the "Frontier Guards," hurriedly organized at Hunter's request by the cunning, ambitious, violence-prone Jim Lane, senator-elect from Kansas.[5] Consisting of about fifty men, the Guards on April 18 took up residence in the White House. A member

47

of the Guard wrote home describing how he and his colleagues "slept sweetly on the President's rich Brussels [carpet], with their arms stacked in martial line down the center of the hall, while two long rows of Kansas ex-Governors, Senators, Judges, Editors, Generals and Jayhawkers were dozing upon each side, and the sentinels made regular beats around them." Those guardians were instructed to admit no one to the East Room who failed to give the password. "Even the President," a newspaper reported, "when he attempted to enter the hall, accompanied by his lady and some members of the Cabinet, was pricked with the sharp steel of the sentinel, and told,—perhaps jocosely—that *he could not possibly come in!*"[6] Lincoln "was forced to beat a retreat, to the no small amusement of the company."[7] When the unit was disbanded after a few days, Lincoln said in thanking them that "language was incapable of expressing how great an obligation he and the people all over this country are under to this little patriotic band of men, for their timely services in preventing, as they undoubtedly did prevent, this capital from falling into the hands of the enemy."[8]

Immediately after the fall of Fort Sumter, anxiety mounted steadily as disaster followed disaster.[9] On April 17, Virginia seceded; on the 18th, Federal troops abandoned Harper's Ferry at the northern entrance to the vital Shenandoah Valley, torching the armory as they left; on the 20th, Union forces set afire the Gosport Navy Yard in Norfolk before evacuating it. Rumors circulated that fifteen hundred Confederates in Alexandria were poised to attack the capital, seven miles to the north.[10]

Lincoln found it hard to credit rumors that Virginia had left the Union so precipitously. On April 17, when he learned of the Old Dominion's secession, he "said he was not yet prepared to believe that one of the founders of the Union, and the mother of so many of its rulers, was yet ready to break down her own work and blast her own glorious history by this act of treason."[11]

Relieving the tension slightly was the arrival of five unarmed companies of Pennsylvania militiamen at the capital on April 18.[12] Accompanied by Cameron and Seward, Lincoln visited them at the Capitol to express his hearty thanks for their promptitude as well as "his great relief and satisfaction at their presence."[13] One soldier recalled that when the president entered, "[p]rofound silence for a moment resulted, broken by the hand clapping and cheers of the tired volunteers. . . . I remember how I was impressed by the kindliness of his face and awkward hanging of his arms and legs, his apparent bashfulness in the presence of these first soldiers of the Republic, and with it all a grave, rather mournful bearing in his attitude." After observing the men, some of whom were wounded, he said, "I did not come here to make a speech. The time for speech-making has gone by, and the time for action is at hand. I have come here to give the Washington Artillerists from the State of Pennsylvania a warm welcome to the city of Washington and to shake every officer and soldier by the hand, providing you will give me that privilege." As he shook their hands, a "kind of awe seemed to come over the boys."[14]

Nicolay and Hay described the scene at the White House in those anxious first days of the Civil War (*Abraham Lincoln: A History*, 4:105–7):

The events of the week—the daily mustering of volunteers, the preparations for defense, the telegrams from the various State capitals—had thrown Washington into a military fever. The social sympathies of the permanent population of Washington, and especially of its suburbs, Georgetown and Alexandria, were strongly Southern; but the personal interests of its inhabitants and property holders were necessarily bound up with the course and fate of the existing Government.

The Union manifestations were for the moment dominant, and volunteers came forward readily, even with some enthusiasm, to fill up the District quota. The city was also yet full of office-seekers from various States north and west. Cassius M. Clay of Kentucky, and Senator-elect James H. Lane of Kansas, both men of mark and courage, after an evening or two of flaming speech-making, organized them respectively into the "Clay

Battalion" and the "Frontier Guards." These companies, of from thirty to sixty men each, were what might be called irregular volunteers-recruits from East and West, of all ranks in the great army of politics, who came forward to shoulder a musket without enlistment, commission, paymaster, or commissariat.

By this time the danger had become so threatening that every scrap and show of military force was welcome and really useful. The Government furnished them arms, and gave them in charge of Major (afterwards Major-General) David Hunter, who, on the evening of the 18th, stationed Clay's company in Willard's Hall, with orders to patrol the streets, and took Lane's Frontier Guards to the post of honor at the Executive Mansion. At dusk they filed into the famous East Room, clad in citizens' dress, but carrying very new, untarnished muskets, and following Lane, brandishing a sword of irreproachable brightness. Here ammunition boxes were opened and cartridges dealt out; and after spending the evening in an exceedingly rudimentary squad drill, under the light of the gorgeous gas chandeliers, they disposed themselves in picturesque bivouac on the brilliant-patterned velvet carpet—perhaps the most luxurious cantonment which American soldiers have ever enjoyed. Their motley composition, their anomalous surroundings, the extraordinary emergency, their mingled awkwardness and earnestness, rendered the scene a medley of bizarre contradictions, a blending of masquerade and tragedy, of grim humor and realistic seriousness,—a combination of Don Quixote and Daniel Boone altogether impossible to describe. However, their special guardianship of the East Room lasted only for a night or two, until more suitable quarters could be extemporized; and for many days they lent an important moral influence in repressing and overawing the lurking treason still present in a considerable fraction among the Washington inhabitants.

5

WASHINGTON BESIEGED: APRIL 1861

On April 19, 1861, the anniversary of the 1775 Battle of Lexington, where Massachusetts men were the first to be killed in the Revolutionary War, members of the Sixth Massachusetts regiment were the first to die in the Civil War when a mob attacked them as they passed through Baltimore.[1] Shots were exchanged, killing four soldiers and wounding thirty-six others; in addition, twelve civilians were killed and scores wounded.[2] The North howled in outrage, causing residents of the Monumental City to become "greatly depressed by forebodings of the terrible retribution in store for them."[3]

When informed of the attack on the Massachusetts Sixth, Lincoln "was very much astonished" and said that Maryland Governor Thomas H. Hicks "had assured him, the day before, that the troops would have no trouble in passing through Baltimore, and that if they wanted any troops from Washington he (Gov. Hicks) would telegraph." When Hicks wired saying "Send no more troops," the president assumed that the governor wanted no help from the administration "and that he would take care and see that the troops passed safely."[4] (In fact, on April 18 Governor Hicks and Baltimore Mayor George W. Brown telegraphed Lincoln, "Send no troops here." They repeated that message the following day.)[5]

When two leading citizens of the Monumental City expressed fear that indignant Northerners might swarm into the Free State, Lincoln "most solemnly reassured them that there was no danger. 'Our people are easily influenced by reason. They have determined to prosecute this matter with energy but with the most temperate spirit. You are entirely safe from lawless invasion.'"[6]

Upon the arrival of the Massachusetts Sixth in Washington, Lincoln greeted its commander, Colonel Edward F. Jones, warmly: "Thank God, you have come; for if you had not Washington would have been in the hands of the rebels before morning."[7] Observing their shabby uniforms, the president directed that the troops be given regular army shirts and trousers.[8]

After midnight, when a delegation from Baltimore arrived at the White House to make an appeal like Hicks's, Nicolay refused to wake the president but called on the secretary of war, who indicated no interest in complying with their request. The next morning Lincoln encountered the Baltimoreans as he descended the White House stairs to confer with General Scott, who urged that reinforcements be sent around rather than through Baltimore. The president, "always inclined to give all men credit for fairness and sincerity," agreed to this compromise solution, thus satisfying the committee. Half in jest, he told them that "if I grant you this, you will come to-morrow demanding that no troops shall pass around."[9]

Lincoln then wired Hicks and Brown, summoning them to Washington for a consultation. Around midnight a telegram arrived from Brown stating that Hicks was unavailable and asking if he should come alone. At 1 A.M., Nicolay woke Lincoln, who had his secretary reply to the mayor, "Come."[10]

On April 20, Lincoln also met with Maryland Congressmen Anthony Kennedy and J. Morrison Harris, who repeated the message of the previous Baltimore callers. Impatiently, Lincoln declared, "My God, Mr. Harris, I don't know what to make of your people. You have sent me one committee already, and they seemed to be perfectly satisfied with what I said to them." When Harris insisted that no more troops pass through his state, the president answered, "My God, Sir, what am I to do? I had better go out and hang myself on the first tree I come to, than to give up the power of the Federal Government in this way. I don't want to go through your town, or near it, if I can help it; but we must have the troops here to relieve ourselves, or we shall die like rats in a heap." Lincoln then chided Harris for abandoning his Republican principles.[11]

Sunday, April 21, was a "dreary and anxious" day at the White House.[12] That morning, Brown and several of his fellow townsmen fulfilled Lincoln's prediction by demanding "in the most earnest manner" that no troops pass through their state at all! The president at first balked, asserting "with great earnestness" that the protection of Washington "was the sole object of concentrating troops there, and he protested that none of the troops brought through Maryland were intended for any purposes hostile to the State, or aggressive as against Southern States." The delegation left, reassured of the president's desire to avoid further bloodshed in the Free State. But upon reaching the depot to return home, they received word that Pennsylvania reinforcements had recently arrived in Cockeysville, fifteen miles north of Baltimore, throwing that city into a panic. Indignantly the delegation returned to the White House to insist that those troops be sent back to the Keystone State. Fearing that renewed hostilities between soldiers and civilians might play into the hands of Maryland's secessionists and that a pitched battle in the City of Monuments would delay the arrival of reinforcements, Lincoln ordered the recall of those forces.[13]

Many Unionists were "not only wounded but sickened" by this order, including some cabinet members.[14] Gideon Welles, at a meeting held soon after the Baltimoreans finally departed, "jumped up, swung his hat under his arm and hastily walked out, telling them if that was their policy *he* would have no responsibility in the matter."[15] With characteristic belligerence, Seward "said the treason of Hicks would not surprise him—that the Seventh [New York regiment] could cut their way through three thousand rioters—that Baltimore delenda est [i.e., must be destroyed]."[16] In Pennsylvania, Andrew Reeder observed that the "report made by the Mayor of Balt. of his interview with the Presdt I am sorry to say has excited a good deal of indignation and if he tells the truth, the bearing of the Presidt. was too weak and lowly for the commander in chief to use to the representative of rebels."[17] An American residing in Switzerland said "I felt pained for my country when I read an account" of the president's interview.[18] The New York *Tribune* scornfully called Lincoln's decision "the height of Quixotic scrupulosity," and the *Times* went so far as to suggest that the president be impeached.[19] Lincoln dismissed these press critics, saying "we can afford to pass them by with the dying words of the Massachusetts statesman [Daniel Webster], 'we still live.' I am sure they don't worry me any, and I reckon they don't benefit the parties who write them."[20] (Privately he was less stoical, calling the articles "villainous.")[21] Months later, when asked it he had read an editorial in a certain New York newspaper—probably the *Morning Express*—he replied, "No, I dare not open that paper. I'd like now and then to see its editorials, for the fun of the thing, but if I do I'm sure to get seduced into reading its Washington dispatches—and then *my sleep is gone for one night at least.*"[22]

Baltimore secessionists also expressed their displeasure, evidently "disgusted" with Lincoln's "familiarity and want of dignity."[23] The head of one delegation, the Rev. Dr. Richard Fuller, who was both a large-scale slave owner and a prominent Baptist minister, snorted that Lincoln "is wholly inaccessible to Christian appeals—& his egotism will forever prevent his comprehending what patriotism means." From the president "nothing is to be hoped."[24]

To those protesting his decision, Lincoln explained that he had gone out of his way, "as an exhaustion of the means of conciliation & kindness," to accommodate the Baltimore authorities who protested that they had insufficient power to guarantee the safety of Union troops passing through their city but could assure undisturbed passage elsewhere in Maryland. He added that "this was the last time he was going to interfere in matters of strictly military concernment" and that "he would leave them hereafter wholly to military men."[25]

On April 22, when yet another group from Baltimore called to demand that no troops be allowed to pass through the Free State and that the Confederacy be recognized, the president lost his customary patience. With some asperity he scolded them:

> You, gentlemen, come here to me and ask for peace on any terms, and yet have no word of condemnation for those who are making war on us. You express great horror of bloodshed, and yet would not lay a straw in the way of those who are organizing in Virginia and elsewhere to capture this city. The rebels attack Fort Sumter, and your citizens attack troops sent to the defense of the Government, and the lives and property in Washington, and yet you would have me break my oath and surrender the Government without a blow. There is no Washington in that—no Jackson in that—no manhood nor honor in that.

Lincoln insisted that he had "no desire to invade the South; but I must have the troops, and mathematically the necessity exists that they should come through Maryland. They can't crawl under the earth, and they can't fly over it. Why, sir, those Carolinians are now crossing Virginia to come here to hang me, and what can I do?" He added that "he must run the machine as he found it." There would be no need for a clash as Union soldiers crossed Maryland: "Now, sir, if you won't hit me, I won't hit you!" But if those troops were forcibly resisted, "*I will lay Baltimore in ashes.*" When told that 75,000 Marylanders would resist the passage of Union troops, he promptly and decidedly "replied that he presumed there was room enough on her soil to bury 75,000 men." As the delegation left, Lincoln said to one young member of it, "You have heard of the Irishman who, when a fellow was cutting his throat with a blunt razor, complained that he haggled it. Now, if I can't have troops directly through Maryland, and must have them all the way round by water, or marched across out-of-the-way territory, I shall be haggled."[26]

Lincoln's anger at Baltimoreans persisted. In September, when Mayor Brown was arrested for aiding the rebels, a delegation from the Monumental City pleaded for his release. The president replied, "I believe, gentlemen, if we arrested Jeff. Davis, committees would wait upon me and represent him to be a Union man." He recounted a conversation he had had with Brown in the spring during which that official had shown sympathy for the Confederacy. "I have not heard of any act of mayor Brown since, which would lead to the belief that he was in favor of supporting the Government to put down this rebellion."[27]

The reigning literary lion in the City of Monuments, John Pendelton Kennedy, accurately predicted that "this refusal of a right of transit will arouse the whole North."[28] Throughout the Free States, people declared that if troops could not pass through Baltimore, the "city and its name should be swept from the face of the earth."[29] In Ohio, a leading Methodist circuit rider insisted that "Maryland must be kept open" even it meant that "we make it a graveyard."[30] Former Kansas governor Andrew H. Reeder told Simon Cameron, "If Baltimore was laid in ashes the North would rejoice over it and laud the Spirit that dictated the act."[31] A correspondent for the New York *Tribune* asked, *apropos* of Lincoln's order sending the Pennsylvania troops home, "Is not this enough to make one's blood boil? We are not allowed to defend our Capital, or our wives and children."[32] Albert D. Richardson said of Baltimore, "*That city has stood long enough.*" It "should be razed to the earth, and not one stone left upon another."[33] Richardson's boss, Horace Greeley, argued that if "the passage of our armies be disputed over our own highways, and if Senators of the United States have to steal away privily to escape being torn to pieces by the inhabitants of Baltimore," then "the sooner that city be burned with fire and leveled to the earth, and made an abode for owls and satyrs, and a place for fishermen to dry their nets, the better."[34] Chase urged the president to deal firmly with Maryland in order to avoid any "new humiliation" such as the possible seizure of Fort McHenry.[35]

When a leading Maryland Unionist, Reverdy Johnson, warned that the people of his state and Virginia feared the troops headed for Washington would invade the South, Lincoln denied any such intent. On April 24, he assured the former senator that "the sole purpose of bringing troops *here* is to defend this capital. . . . I have no purpose to *invade* Virginia, with them or any other troops, as I understand the word *invasion*. But suppose Virginia sends her troops, or admits others through her borders, to assail this capital, am I not to repel them, even to the crossing of the Potomac if I can? Suppose Virginia erects, or permits to be erected, batteries on the opposite shore, to bombard the city, are we to stand still and see it done? In a word, if Virginia strikes us, are we not to strike back, and as effectively as we can? Again, are we not to hold Fort Monroe (for instance) if we can? I have no objection to declare a thousand times that I have no purpose to *invade* Virginia or any other State, but I do not mean to let them invade us without striking back."[36]

Meanwhile, Washington had become isolated from the North. On April 20, Maryland officials ordered the destruction of bridges on rail lines connecting the capital with Baltimore. Telegraph wires were cut, and mail service to the District ceased. Troops heading there, among them the Seventh New York and the First Rhode Island regiments, were held up for several days as they sought alternate routes. Later the president remarked, "He who strangles himself, for whatever motive, is not more unreasonable than were those citizens of Baltimore who, in a single night, destroyed the Baltimore and Ohio railroad, the Northern Central railroad, and the railroad from Baltimore to Philadelphia."[37]

Compounding the president's woes were the resignations of about one third of the officers in the army and navy.[38] Especially disconcerting was the case of Colonel John B. Magruder, commander of the Washington garrison, who on April 18 had told Lincoln, "Sir, I was brought up and educated under the glorious old flag. I have lived under it and have fought under it, and, sir, with the help of God, I shall fight under it again and, if need be, shall die under it." The president replied, "[Y]ou are an officer of the army and a Southern gentleman, and incapable of any but honorable conduct." Lincoln added that "independently of all other reasons he felt it to be a constitutional obligation binding upon his conscience to put down secession" even though "he bore testimony to the honor, good faith, and high character of the Southern people, whom he 'knew well.'" Three days thereafter the colonel announced his intention of quitting the service to join the Confederacy. Later Lincoln said that he could not remember "any single event of my administration that gave me so much pain or wounded me so deeply as the singular behavior of Colonel Magruder." To the president "it seemed the more wanton and cruel in him because he knew that I had implicit confidence in his integrity. The fact is, when I learned that he had gone over to the enemy and I had been so completely deceived in him, my confidence was shaken in everybody, and I hardly knew who to trust anymore."[39] More significantly, Colonel Robert E. Lee spurned an offer from Lincoln (unofficially conveyed through Francis P. Blair Sr.) to command the Union army. "Mr Blair," said the army's most capable officer, "I look upon secession as anarchy—if I owned the four millions of slaves in the South I would sacrifice them all to the Union—but how can I draw my sword upon Virginia, my native State?"[40] On April 23, Lee accepted command of the military forces of the Old Dominion. In July, Lincoln publicly remarked that it was

worthy of note, that while in this, the government's hour of trial, large numbers of those in the Army and Navy, who have been favored with the offices, have resigned, and proved false to the hand which had pampered them, not one common soldier, or common sailor is known to have deserted his flag. Great honor is due to those officers who remain true, despite the example of their treacherous associates; but the greatest honor, and most important fact of all is, the unanimous firmness of the common soldiers and common sailors. To the last man, so far as known, they have successfully resisted the traitorous efforts of those, whose commands, but an hour before, they obeyed as absolute law. This is the patriotic instinct of the plain people. They understand, without an argument, that destroying the government, which was made by Washington, means no good to them.[41]

In Washington, April 24 was "a day of gloom and doubt," when everyone seemed "filled with a vague distrust and recklessness."[42] Washingtonians not only feared a Confederate attack but also worried that the "the suspense and uncertainty" among the population had grown "to such a pitch that a very small untoward circumstance or accident" might touch off rioting or panic. The two thousand troops in Washington afforded some comfort, but it was feared that the three-thousand-man District Militia might prove disloyal, and then, Nicolay speculated, "we would have to look down the muzzles of our own guns."[43] Hence, despite criticism, Lincoln refused to call up the local militia. Hotels emptied as people fled to safety outside Washington, while those who remained began girding for a siege.[44] And the threat of famine hung over the city as flour supplies dwindled.[45]

A day later the thick gloom blanketing the capital suddenly lifted as the New York Seventh arrived to thunderous cheers. Lincoln and Seward greeted them at the Navy Yard, shaking hands all around. One soldier recalled that the president showed a "serious and almost fatherly demeanor" as "he bent slightly in taking our hands. . . . Indeed one hand was not enough to express his feeling, and with his left he took each of us by the elbow and gave a hearty pressure." As the troops marched past the White House, Lincoln, who was described as "the happiest-looking man in town," reportedly "smiled all over."[46]

Nicolay and Hay describe the tension in Washington during those anxious April days (*Abraham Lincoln: A History*, 4:130–32, 140–57):

*T*hrough all of Friday night and Saturday [April 19 and 20] the secession feeling steadily rose in Baltimore; the city, to the full extent of its ability, made ready to resist by force the further passage of troops; and to a considerable degree the same excitement, and the same resolve and preparation, spread like wildfire to the country villages of Maryland. Through various delays it happened that Mayor Brown did not reach Washington until Sunday morning, April 21, in obedience to Lincoln's request of the previous afternoon. The mayor brought with him two members of the first Baltimore committee, and besides these a prominent and active secessionist.

Naturally, Mayor Brown and his committee-men, while they carefully kept secret their own official bridge-burning, did not undercolor their description of this insurrectionary mood of their people. The discussion was participated in by General Scott and the Cabinet, and took a wide range, lasting all Sunday forenoon (April 21). The President insisted that troops must come. General Scott explained that they could only come in one of three ways: first, through Baltimore; second, by the Harrisburg route and a march round Baltimore; and third, by the Annapolis route. The last two routes were therefore agreed upon.

General Scott said if the people would permit them to go by either of these routes uninterrupted, the necessity of their passing through Baltimore would be avoided. If the people would not permit them a transit thus remote from the city, they must select their own best route, and, if need be, fight their way through Baltimore, a result which he earnestly deprecated. The President expressed his hearty concurrence in the desire to avoid a collision, and said that no more troops should be ordered through Baltimore if they were permitted to go uninterrupted by either of the other routes suggested. In this disposition the Secretary of War expressed his participation.

Mayor Brown agreed to the arrangement, and promised on his part "that the city authorities would use all lawful means to prevent their citizens from leaving Baltimore to attack the troops in passing at a distance."

With this agreement they took their leave, and the President proceeded to other business, when, to his astonishment, Mayor Brown and his companions again made their appearance, between two and three o'clock in the afternoon. They brought a sensational telegram just received by them from Mr. Garrett, president of the Baltimore and Ohio Railroad, which read: "Three thousand Northern troops are reported to be at Cockeysville; intense excitement prevails; churches have been dismissed, and the people are arming in mass. To prevent terrific bloodshed, the result of your interview and arrangement is awaited."

Cockeysville is on the Harrisburg route, fifteen miles from Baltimore; and because they had no previous notice of such approach, the committee now intimated that advantage had been taken of their presence in Washington to bring these forces within striking distance of Baltimore. The Cabinet and Scott were again summoned, and the whole discussion was opened up anew.

The President, at once, in the most decided way urged the recall of the troops, saying that he had no idea they would be there to-day; lest there should be the slightest suspicion of bad faith on his part in summoning the mayor to Washington, and allowing troops to march on the city during his absence, he desired that the troops should, if it were practicable, be sent back at once to York or Harrisburg.

Orders were accordingly issued to this effect, the President, however, notifying the committee that he should not again in any wise interfere with the military entanglements. In this, as in his Sumter policy, Lincoln interposed his authority to exercise the utmost liberality and forbearance. He did not expect to appease the Maryland rebels, but to make them clearly responsible for further bloodshed, should any occur, and thereby to hold the Maryland Unionists. These were sufficient motives; and underlying them he had yet another, still more conclusive. All this examination of maps and discussion had brought the conviction to his quick penetration, in advance of any of his councilors, that the Harrisburg route was, in the present state of affairs, entirely impracticable and useless. . . .

Washington now began to take on some of the aspects of a siege. The large stores of flour and grain at the Georgetown mills, and even that already loaded for shipment on schooners, were seized, and long trains of carts were engaged in removing it to safer storage in the public buildings. Prices of provisions were rising. The little passenger steamers plying on the Potomac were taken possession of by the military officers to be used for guard and picket duty on the river. The doors, windows, and stairways of the public buildings were protected by barricades, and the approaches to them guarded by sentinels. All travel and nearly all business came to a standstill, and theaters and places of amusement were closed.

With the first notice of the burning of the railroad bridges, the strangers, visitors, and transient sojourners in the city became possessed of an uncontrollable desire to get away. So long as the trains ran to Baltimore, they proceeded to that point; from there they sought to escape northward by whatever chances of transportation offered themselves. By some of these fugitives the Government had taken the precaution to send duplicates of important orders and dispatches to Northern cities. This *sauve qui peut* quickly denuded Washington of its redundant population. While the Unionist non-combatants were flying northward, the secessionists were making quite as hurried an escape to the South; for it was strongly rumored that the Government intended to impress the whole male population of Washington into military service for the defense of the city.

One incidental benefit grew out of the panic—the Government was quickly relieved of its treasonable servants. Some hundreds of clerks resigned out of the various departments on this Monday, April 22, and the impending danger not only brought these to final decision, but also many officers of high grades and important functions. Commodore Franklin Buchanan, in charge of the Washington navy yard, together with nearly all his subordinate officers, suddenly discovered their unwillingness longer to keep their oaths and serve the United States; and that night this invaluable navy depot, with all its vast stores of material, its immense workshops and priceless machinery, was intrusted solely to the loyalty and watchfulness of Commander John A. Dahlgren and a little handful of marines, scarcely enough in number to have baffled half a dozen adroit incendiaries, or to ascertain the street gossip outside the walls of the establishment.

Among the scores of army and navy resignations reported the same day was that of Captain John B. Magruder, 1st Artillery, then in command of a light battery on which General Scott had placed special reliance for the defense of Washington. No single case of defection gave Lincoln such astonishment and pain as this one. "Only three days ago," he said, when the fact was made known to him, "Magruder came voluntarily to me in this room, and with his own lips and in my presence repeated over and over again his asseverations and protestations of loyalty and fidelity."

It was not merely the loss of an officer, valuable and necessary though he might be in the emergency, but the significance of this crowning act of perfidy which troubled the President, and to the suggestiveness of which he could not close his eyes. Was there not only no patriotism left, but was all sense of personal obligation, of everyday honesty, and of manliness of character gone also? Was everything crumbling at his touch? In whom should he place confidence? To whom should he give orders, if clerks, and captains, and commodores, and quartermaster-generals, and governors of States, and justices of the Supreme Court proved false in the moment of need? If men of the character and rank of the Magruders, the Buchanans, the [Charles S.] McCauleys, the [Robert E.] Lees, the [Joseph E.] Johnstons, the [Samuel] Coopers, the [John A.] Campbells were giving way, where might he not fear treachery? There was certainly no danger that all the officers of the Government would thus prove recreant; but might not the failure of a single one bearing an important trust cause a vital and irreparable disaster?

The perplexities and uncertainties of the hour are set forth with frank brevity by General Scott, in the report which was sent to the President that night of Monday, April 22:

> I have but little that is certain to report, viz.: *First,* That there are three or four steamers off Annapolis, with volunteers for Washington; *Second,* That their landing will be opposed by the citizens, reënforced from Baltimore; *Third,* That the landing may be effected nevertheless by good

management; and *Fourth,* That the rails on the Annapolis
road (twenty miles) have been taken up. Several efforts to
communicate with those troops to-day have failed; but three
other detached persons are repeating the attempt, and one or
more of them will, I think, succeed. Once ashore, the regiments (if but two, and there are probably more) would have
no difficulty in reaching Washington on foot, other than
the want of wagons to transport camp equipage; and the
quartermaster that I have sent there (I do not know that he
has arrived) has orders to hire wagons if he can, and if not,
to impress, etc. Of rumors, the following are probable, viz.:
First, That from 1500 to 2000 troops are at the White House
(four miles below Mount Vernon, a narrow point in the Potomac) engaged in erecting a battery; *Second,* That an equal
force is collected or in progress of assemblage on the two
sides of the river to attack Fort Washington; and *Third,* That
extra cars went up yesterday to bring down from Harper's
Ferry about 2000 other troops to join in a general attack on
this capital—that is, on many of its fronts at once. I feel con-
fident that with our present forces we can defend the Capitol,
the Arsenal, and all the executive buildings (seven) against
10,000 troops not better than our district volunteers.

Tuesday [April 23] morning came, but no news from Annapolis, no volunteers up the Potomac. It was Cabinet day;
and about noon, after the President and his councilors were
assembled, messengers announced the arrival of two steamers at the navy yard. There was a momentary hope that these
might be the long-expected ships from New York; but inquiries proved them to be the [warship] *Pawnee* and a transport
on their return from the expedition to Norfolk. The worst
apprehensions concerning that important post were soon realized—it was irretrievably lost. The only bit of comfort to
be derived from the affair was that the vessels brought back
a number of marines and sailors, who would now add a little
fraction of strength to the defense of the capital. The officers
of the expedition were soon before the President and Cabinet,
and related circumstantially the tale of disaster and destruction

which the treachery of a few officers and the credulity of the commandant had rendered unavoidable.

The Gosport navy yard, at Norfolk, Virginia, was of such value and importance that its safety, from the very beginning of Mr. Lincoln's Administration, had neither been overlooked nor neglected. But, like every other exposed or threatened point,— like Sumter, Pickens, Tortugas, Key West, Fort Monroe, Baltimore, Harper's Ferry, and Washington itself,—its fate was involved in the want of an army and navy of adequate strength. The day the President resolved on the Sumter expedition, 250 seamen had been ordered from Brooklyn to Norfolk to render Gosport more safe. Instead of going there, it was thought necessary to change their destination to Sumter and Pickens. And so, though the danger to Gosport was not lost sight of, the reënforcements to ward it off were never available.

The officers of the navy yard were outwardly loyal; the commandant had grown gray in the service of his country, and enjoyed the full confidence of his equals and superiors. It was known that the secessionists had designs upon the post; but it was believed that the watchfulness which had been ordered and the measures of precaution which had been arranged under the special supervision of two trusted officers of the Navy Department, who were carrying out the personal instructions of Secretary Welles, would meet the danger. At a critical moment, Commandant Charles S. McCauley committed a fatal mistake. The subordinate officers of the yard, professing loyalty, practiced treason, and lured him into their designs. Several valuable vessels lay at the navy yard. To secure them eventually for Virginia, Governor [John] Letcher had, among his first acts of hostility, attempted to obstruct the channel from Norfolk to Fort Monroe by means of sunken vessels. But the effort failed; the passage still remained practicable. Ascertaining this, Commodore James Alden and Chief Engineer Benjamin F. Isherwood, specially sent for the task by Secretary [of the Navy Gideon] Welles, had, with the help of the commandant of the yard, prepared the best ships—the *Merrimac,* the *Germantown,* the *Plymouth,* and the *Dolphin*—for quick removal to Fort Monroe. The engines of the *Merrimac* were put in order, the fires under her boilers were lighted, the moment of her departure had been announced, when suddenly a change came over the spirit of Commandant McCauley. Virginia passed her ordinance of secession; the traitorous officers of the navy yard were about to throw off their mask and desert their flag; and, as a parting stroke of intrigue, they persuaded the commandant that he must retain the *Merrimac* for the security of the yard. Yielding to this treacherous advice, he countermanded her permission to depart and ordered her fires to be put out. Thus baffled, Isherwood and Alden hastened back to Washington to obtain the superior orders of the Secretary over this most unexpected and astounding action.

They reached Washington on this errand respectively on the 18th and 19th of April, just at the culminating point of insurrection and danger. Hasty consultations were held and energetic orders were issued. The *Pawnee,* just returned from her Sumter cruise, was again coaled, supplied, and fitted out—processes consuming precious hours but which could not be omitted. On the evening of April 19 she steamed down the Potomac under command of Commodore Hiram Paulding, with discretionary orders to defend or to destroy. Next evening, April 20, having landed at Fort Monroe and taken on board three to five hundred men of the Third Massachusetts, only that morning arrived from Boston, and who embarked without a single ration, the *Pawnee* proceeded to Norfolk, passing without difficulty through the seven sunken hulks in the Elizabeth River. But Commodore Paulding was too late. The commandant, once more successfully plied with insidious advice, had yielded to the second suggestion of his juniors, and had scuttled the removable ships—ostensibly to prevent their being seized and used by the rebels. As they were slowly sinking, no effort to remove them could succeed, and no resource was left but to destroy everything so far as could be done. Accordingly, there being bright moonlight, the greater part of Saturday night was devoted to the work of destruction. Several parties were detailed to fire the ships and the buildings and to lay a mine to blow up the dry-dock, and the sky was soon lighted by an immense conflagration.

Yet, with all this effort, the sacrifice was left incomplete. Not more than half the buildings were consumed. The workshops, with their valuable machinery, escaped. The 1500 to 2000 heavy cannon in the yard could neither be removed nor rendered unserviceable. Some unforeseen accident finally prevented the explosion of the dry-dock. Of the seven ships burned to the water's edge, the hull of the *Merrimac* was soon afterwards raised, and in the course of events changed by the rebels into the ironclad *Merrimac,* or, as they named her, the *Virginia.* At five o'clock on Sunday morning the *Pawnee* considered her work finished, and steamed away from Gosport, followed by the sailing-ship *Cumberland.*

No point of peril had been so clearly foreseen, and apparently so securely guarded against, as the loss of the three or four valuable ships at Norfolk; and yet, in spite of foresight and precaution, they had gone to worse than ruin through the same train of circumstances which had lost Sumter and permitted the organization of the Montgomery rebellion. The loss of ships and guns was, however, not all; behind these was the damaging moral effect upon the Union cause and feeling.

For four consecutive days each day had brought a great disaster—Virginia's secession on the 17th; the burning of Harper's Ferry on the 18th; the Baltimore riot and destruction of railroad bridges on the 19th; the abandonment and destruction of the great navy yard and its ships on the night of the 20th. This began to look like an irresistible current of fate. No popular sentiment could long stem such a tide of misfortune. The rebels of Virginia, Maryland, and especially of Washington began to feel that Providence wrought in their behalf, and that their conspiracy was already crowned with success. Evidently with such a feeling, on this same Tuesday [April 23], Associate Justice John A. Campbell, still a member of the Supreme Court and under oath to support the Constitution of the United States, again sent a letter of aid and comfort to Jefferson Davis. He wrote:

> Maryland is the object of chief anxiety with the North and
> the Administration. Their fondest hope will be to command
> the Chesapeake and relieve this capital. Their pride and their

fanaticism would be sadly depressed by a contrary issue. This will be the great point of contest in all negotiations. . . . I incline to think that they are prepared to abandon the south of the Potomac. But not beyond. Maryland is weak. She has no military men of talents, and I did hear that Colonel [Benjamin] Huger was offered command and declined it—however, his resignation had not been accepted. Huger is plainly not competent for such a purpose. Lee is in Virginia. Think of the condition of Baltimore and provide for it, for there is the place of danger. The events at Baltimore have placed a new aspect upon everything to the North. There is a perfect storm there. While it has to be met, no unnecessary addition should be made to increase it.

Another night of feverish public unrest, another day of anxiety to the President—Wednesday, April 24. There was indeed no attack on the city; but, on the other hand, no arrival of troops to place its security beyond doubt. Repetition of routine duties; repetition of unsubstantial rumors; long faces in the streets; a holiday quiet over the city; closed shutters and locked doors of business houses; the occasional clatter of a squad of cavalry from point to point; sentinels about the departments; sentinels about the Executive Mansion; Willard's Hotel, which a week before was swarming with busy crowds, now deserted as if smitten by a plague, with only furtive servants to wake echoes along the vacant corridors—an oppressive contrast to the throng of fashion and beauty which had so lately made it a scene of festivity from midday to midnight.

Ever since the telegraph stopped on Sunday night, the Washington operators had been listening for the ticking of their instruments, and had occasionally caught fugitive dispatches passing between Maryland secessionists, which were for the greater part immediately known to be untrustworthy; for General Scott kept up a series of military scouts along the Baltimore railroad as far as Annapolis Junction, twenty miles from Washington, from which point a branch railroad ran at a right angle to the former, twenty miles to Annapolis, on Chesapeake Bay.

The general dared not risk a detachment permanently to hold the junction; no considerable secession force had been encountered, and the railroad was yet safe. But it was known, or at least strongly probable, that the volunteers from the North had been at Annapolis since Sunday morning. Why did they not land? Why did they not advance? The Annapolis road was known to be damaged; but could they not march twenty miles?

The previous day (April 23) had, by some lucky chance, brought a New York mail three days old. The newspapers in it contained breezy premonitions of the Northern storm—Anderson's enthusiastic reception; the departure of the Seventh New York regiment; the sailing of Governor [William] Sprague with his Rhode Islanders; the monster meeting in Union Square [in New York city], with the outpouring of half a million of people in processions and listening to speeches from half a dozen different stands; the energetic measures of the New York Common Council; the formation of the Union Defense Committee; whole columns of orders and proclamations; the flag-raisings; the enlistments; the chartering and freighting of ships; and from all quarters news of the wild, jubilant uprising of the whole immense population of the free States. All this was gratifying, pride-kindling, reassuring; and yet, read and re-read with avidity in Washington that day, it would always bring after it the galling reflection that all this magnificent outburst of patriotism was paralyzed by the obstacle of a twenty miles' march between Annapolis and the junction. Had the men of the North no legs?

Lincoln, by nature and habit so calm, so equable, so undemonstrative, nevertheless passed this period of interrupted communication and isolation from the North in a state of nervous tension which put all his great powers of mental and physical endurance to their severest trial. General Scott's reports, though invariably expressing his confidence in successful defense, frankly admitted the evident danger; and the President, with his acuteness of observation and his rapidity and correctness of inference, lost no single one of the external indications of doubt and apprehension. Day after day prediction failed and hope was deferred; troops did not come, ships did not arrive, railroads remained broken, messengers failed to reach their destination. That fact itself demonstrated that he was environed by the un-known—and that whether a Union or a Secession army would first reach the capital was at best an uncertainty.

To a coarse or vulgar nature such a situation would have brought only one of two feelings, either overpowering personal fear, or overweening bravado. But Lincoln, almost a giant in physical stature and strength, combined in his intellectual na-ture a masculine courage and power of logic with an ideal sen-sitiveness of conscience and a sentimental tenderness as delicate as a woman's. This Presidential trust which he had assumed was to him not a mere regalia of rank and honor. Its terrible duties and responsibilities seemed rather a coat of steel armor, heavy to bear, and cutting remorselessly into the quick flesh. That one of the successors of Washington should find himself even to this degree in the hands of his enemies was personally humiliating; but that the majesty of a great nation should be thus insulted and its visible symbols of authority be placed in jeopardy; above all, that the hitherto glorious example of the republic to other nations should stand in this peril of surprise and possible sudden collapse, the Constitution be scoffed, and human freedom become a by-word and reproach—this must have begot in him an anxiety approaching torture.

In the eyes of his countrymen and of the world he was holding the scales of national destiny; he alone knew that for the moment the forces which made the beam vibrate with such uncertainty were beyond his control. In others' society he gave no sign of these inner emotions. But once, on the afternoon of the 23d, the business of the day being over, the Executive of-fice deserted, after walking the floor alone in silent thought for nearly half an hour, he stopped and gazed long and wistfully out of the window down the Potomac in the direction of the expected ships; and, unconscious of other presence in the room, at length broke out with irrepressible anguish in the repeated exclamation, "Why don't they come! Why don't they come!"

One additional manifestation of this bitterness of soul occurred on the day following, though in a more subdued manner. The wounded soldiers of the Sixth Massachusetts, including several officers, came to pay a visit to the President. They were a little shy when they entered the room—having the traditional New England awe of authorities and rulers. Lincoln received them with sympathetic kindness which put them at ease after the interchange of the first greetings. His words of sincere thanks for their patriotism and their suffering, his warm praise of their courage, his hearty recognition of their great service to the public, and his earnestly expressed confidence in their further devotion, quickly won their trust. He spoke to them of the position and prospect of the city, contrasting their prompt arrival with the unexplained delay which seemed to have befallen the regiments supposed to be somewhere on their way from the various States. Pursuing this theme, he finally fell into a tone of irony to which only intense feeling ever drove him. "I begin to believe," said he, "that there is no North. The Seventh regiment is a myth. Rhode Island is another. You are the only real thing." There are few parchment brevets as precious as such a compliment, at such a time, from such a man.

However much the tardiness of the Annapolis reënforcements justified the President's sarcasm, they were at last actually approaching. We left [Massachusetts General Benjamin F.] Butler engaged in assisting the school-ship *Constitution* to a more secure position. The aid proved effectual; but the day's work ended by the ferryboat *Maryland,* with the Eighth Massachusetts still on board, getting hard aground in the shoal water of Annapolis harbor. In this helpless predicament, with nothing to eat but hard pilot-bread and raw salt pork furnished from the *Constitution,* and with no water to drink, the regiment passed the night of Sunday. Early next morning (Monday, April 22) the *Boston* arrived, bringing the Seventh New York; and thus these two regiments, so lately parted at Philadelphia, were once more united. Colonel [Marshall] Lefferts had proceeded on his independent course to Fort Monroe; but receiving no intelligence concerning the Potomac route, concluded, after all, to adopt the more prudent plan of steaming up Chesapeake Bay to Annapolis.

The *Boston* at once set to work, but without eventual success, to pull the *Maryland* into deeper water. Meanwhile the officers of the two regiments were holding interviews and correspondence with Commandant [George] Blake of the Naval School on the one hand, and with the Maryland authorities on the other. Governor Hicks, in punctilious assertion of the paramount State sovereignty of Maryland, protested, in writing, against landing the troops. The Mayor of Annapolis joined in the protest; though privately both declared that Maryland was loyal to the Union, and that they would make no military resistance. That afternoon, both regiments were landed. There was yet a certain friction of military jealousy and refusal to cooperate between Butler and Lefferts; both were eager to proceed to Washington, but differed in their plans; and the many and apparently authentic rumors of the opposing force that would meet them from Baltimore caused discussion and delay. They had no transportation, few rations, and little ammunition. Butler took the first practical measures, by ordering the railroad depot and buildings to be occupied. Here an old locomotive was found, the machinery of which had been carefully disarranged. The mechanical skill of the Yankee militiamen now asserted its value. Private Charles Homans, of the Eighth Massachusetts, at once recognized the locomotive as having been built in "our shop"; and calling to his help several machinists like himself from the Massachusetts regiment, they had no great difficulty in putting it in running order. Tuesday morning (April 23) showing still no warlike demonstrations from any quarter, the surroundings of the town were reconnoitered, and two companies of the Eighth Massachusetts pushed out three and a half miles along the railroad. A beginning was also made towards repairing the track, which was found torn up and displaced here and there. In this work, and in testing the newly repaired locomotive and improvising a train, another day slipped by. In the evening, however, two of the eight messengers sent out from Washington to

Annapolis succeeded in reaching there, the second one bringing the definite orders of General Scott that Butler should remain and hold the place, and that the advancing troops should repair the railroad. That night, also, came four or more steamships with as many additional regiments of volunteers.

Wednesday morning, April 24, being the fourth day at Annapolis for the Eighth Massachusetts and the third for the Seventh New York, they started on their twenty miles' march to the junction. A couple of extemporized platform cars on which the Seventh mounted their little brass howitzers, the patched-up locomotive, and two rickety passenger cars constituted their artillery, baggage, supply, ambulance, and construction train all in one. Thus provided, the two regiments marched, scouted, laid track, and built bridges as occasion required; now fraternizing and cooperating with hearty good-will. It was slow and tedious work; they were not inured to nor provided for even such holiday campaigning as this. Luckily they had fine weather—a warm, sunny, spring day, succeeded by a clear night with a full moon to light it. So they clung pluckily to their duty, hungry and sleepy though they were, all day and all night of Wednesday, and arrived at the junction about daybreak of Thursday. All the previous rumors had taught them that here they might expect a rebel force and fight. The anticipation proved groundless; they learned, on the contrary, that a train from Washington had come to this place for them the day before. It soon again made its appearance; and, quickly embarking on it, by noon the Seventh New York was at its destination.

Those who were in the Federal capital on that Thursday, April 25, will never, during their lives, forget the event. An indescribable gloom had hung over Washington nearly a week, paralyzing its traffic and crushing out its life. As soon as the arrival was known, an immense crowd gathered at the depot to obtain ocular evidence that relief had at length reached the city. Promptly debarking and forming, the Seventh marched up Pennsylvania Avenue to the White House. As they passed up the magnificent street, with their well-formed ranks, their exact military step, their soldierly bearing, their gayly floating flags, and the inspiring music of their splendid regimental band, they seemed to sweep all thought of danger and all taint of treason out of that great national thoroughfare and out of every human heart in the Federal city. The presence of this single regiment seemed to turn the scales of fate. Cheer upon cheer greeted them, windows were thrown up, houses opened, the population came forth upon the streets as for a holiday. It was an epoch in American history. For the first time, the combined spirit and power of Liberty entered the nation's capital.

6

THE FIRST BATTLE OF BULL RUN: JULY 21, 1861

As the spring of 1861 turned to summer and the public pressure for an offensive mounted, Lincoln decided that the Union army must move. Calculating that the fifty thousand Union forces in northern Virginia should be able to defeat the thirty thousand Confederates there, he authorized an offensive. Since many Union soldiers were ninety-day militiamen whose enlistments would soon expire, the president understandably wished to give them "a chance to smell powder before discharging them from service."[1] He may also have believed that to postpone an attack would dispirit the North and perhaps even lead to European recognition of the Confederacy.[2] He was therefore enthusiastic about a plan drawn up at the request of General Winfield Scott, general in chief of all Union armies, by General Irvin McDowell, an abrasive, hypercritical forty-two-year-old gourmand and West Pointer in charge of the Department of Northeastern Virginia. McDowell, whom Quartermaster-General Montgomery Meigs called a "good, brave, commonplace fat man," proposed an attack on Confederate General P. G. T. Beauregard's forces concentrating near Manassas, an important rail junction some thirty miles southwest of Washington.[3] When it was objected that the men needed more training, Lincoln replied that the enemy suffered from the same problem: "You are green, it is true; but they are green, also; you are all green alike."[4] Though accurate, that statement was misleading, for

Union forces would have to maneuver in the presence of an entrenched enemy, a much more complicated challenge than the one the Confederates would face.

On June 25, Lincoln convened a council of war with Scott, Montgomery Meigs, and the cabinet. There the president "expressed a great desire to bag [Confederate forces under Thomas J.] Jackson" at Harper's Ferry, but Scott thought it unfeasible.[5] Four days later at a second council of war, McDowell's fundamentally sound plan was discussed at length, with Meigs countering Scott's vigorous objections.[6] As Meigs recorded in his diary,

> I said that I did not think we would ever end this war without beating
> the rebels; that they had come near us. We were, according to Gen.
> Scott's information, given to us at the Council of the 25th, stronger
> than they, better prepared, our troops better contented, better clothed,
> better fed, better paid, better armed. That we had the most violent of
> the rebels near us; it was better to whip them here than to go far into
> an unhealthy country to fight them, and to fight far from our supplies,
> to spend our money among enemies instead of our friends. To make
> the fight in Virginia was cheaper and better as the case now stood. Let
> them come here to be beaten, and leave the Union men in time to be a
> majority at home.[7]

It was agreed to endorse McDowell's plan, which appeared likely to succeed if the Confederate forces under Joseph E. Johnston in the Shenandoah Valley were unable to join Beauregard. To prevent the two Rebel commands from uniting, Scott ordered General Robert Patterson to hold Johnston in check.[8]

On July 16, after many delays, McDowell lurched toward Manassas, eight days later than the date agreed upon at the council of war. In the oppressive midsummer heat, the raw troops poked along, taking four days to reach their destination, marching poorly, as inadequately trained recruits are wont to do.[9]

As they moved glacially forward, Lincoln grew anxious. A caller on July 19 was struck by his "wearied and worried appearance." During their conversation, the president's "eye-lids dropped repeatedly and he seemed like a person who had been watching with a sick friend and deprived of his wonted sleep."[10]

Beauregard, learning of McDowell's slow advance, appealed for help to Johnston, who easily slipped away from the cautious Patterson and hastened to reinforce his threatened colleague. Upon receiving word of this development, Lincoln asked Scott if it might be advisable to postpone McDowell's attack until Patterson could join him; the general in chief thought that would not be necessary.[11]

On the morning of Sunday, July 21, McDowell's troops splashed across Bull Run and so successfully drove the Confederate left that victory seemed imminent. At noon, Nicolay reported from the White House that "everybody is in great suspense. General Scott talked confidently this morning of success, and very calmly and quietly went to church."[12]

Nicolay and Hay describe the White House on that fateful day (*Abraham Lincoln: A History*, 4:352–55):

*I*t may well be supposed that President Lincoln suffered great anxiety during that eventful Sunday; but General Scott talked confidently of success, and Lincoln bore his impatience without any visible sign, and quietly went to church at eleven o'clock. Soon after noon copies of telegrams began to come to him at the Executive Mansion from the War Department and from army headquarters. They brought, however, no certain information, as they came only from the nearest station to the battlefield, and simply gave what the operator saw and heard. Towards three o'clock they became more frequent, and reported considerable fluctuation in the apparent course and progress of the cannonade. The President went to the office of General Scott, where he found the general asleep, and woke him to talk over the news. Scott said such reports were worth nothing as indications either way, that the changes in the currents of wind and the variation of the echoes made it impossible for a distant listener to determine the course of a battle. He still expressed his confidence in a successful result, and composed himself for another nap when the President left.

Dispatches continued to come about every ten or fifteen minutes, still based on hearing and hearsay; the rumors growing more cheering and definite. They reported that the battle had extended along nearly the whole line; that there had been considerable loss; but that the secession lines had been driven back two or three miles, some of the dispatches said, to the Junction. One of General Scott's aides also brought the telegram of an engineer, repeating that McDowell had driven the enemy before him, that he had ordered the reserves to cross Bull Run, and wanted reënforcements without delay.

The aide further stated substantially that the general was satisfied of the truth of this report, and that McDowell would immediately attack and capture the Junction, perhaps to-night, but certainly by to-morrow noon. Deeming all doubt at an end, President Lincoln ordered his carriage and went out to take his usual evening drive.

He had not returned when, at six o'clock, Secretary Seward came to the Executive Mansion, pale and haggard. "Where is the President?" he asked hoarsely of the private secretaries. "Gone to drive," they answered. "Have you any late news?" he continued. They read him the telegrams which announced victory. "Tell no one," said he. "That is not true. The battle is lost. The telegraph says that McDowell is in full retreat, and calls on General Scott to save the capital. Find the President and tell him to come immediately to General Scott's."

Half an hour later the President returned from his drive, and his private secretaries gave him Seward's message, the first intimation he received of the trying news. He listened in silence, without the slightest change of feature or expression, and walked away to army headquarters. There he read the unwelcome report in a telegram from a captain of engineers: "General McDowell's army in full retreat through Centreville. The day is lost. Save

Washington and the remnants of this army. . . . The routed troops will not re-form." This information was such an irreconcilable contradiction of the former telegram that General Scott utterly refused to believe it. That one officer should report the army beyond Bull Run, driving the enemy and ordering up reserves, and another immediately report it three miles this side of Bull Run, in hopeless retreat and demoralization, seemed an impossibility. Yet the impossible had indeed come to pass; and the apparent change of fortune had been nearly as sudden on the battlefield as in Washington.

The President and the Cabinet met at General Scott's office, and awaited further news in feverish suspense, until a telegram from McDowell confirmed the disaster. Discussion was now necessarily turned to preparation for the future. All available troops were hurried forward to McDowell's support; Baltimore was put on the alert; telegrams were sent to the recruiting stations of the nearest Northern States to lose no time in sending all their organized regiments to Washington; McClellan was ordered to "come down to the Shenandoah Valley with such troops as can be spared from Western Virginia."

A great number of civilians, newspaper correspondents, and several Senators and Representatives had followed McDowell's army to Centreville; Representative Alfred Ely of New York, went to the battlefield itself, and was captured and sent for a long sojourn in Libby Prison at Richmond. Such of these non-combatants as had been fortunate enough to keep their horses and vehicles were the first to reach Washington, arriving about midnight. President Lincoln had returned to the Executive Mansion, and reclining on a lounge in the Cabinet room he heard from several of these eye-witnesses their excited and exaggerated narratives, in which the rush and terror and unseemly stampede of lookers-on and army teamsters were altogether disproportionate and almost exclusive features. The President did not go to his bed that night; morning found him still on his lounge in the executive office, hearing repetitions of these recitals and making memoranda of his own conclusions.

7

LINCOLN AND SECRETARY OF WAR
EDWIN M. STANTON

$\mathcal{L}$incoln's magnanimity, one of the hallmarks of his character, was nowhere more strikingly displayed than in his appointment of Edwin M. Stanton to replace the incompetent, ethically challenged Simon Cameron as secretary of war in January 1862. To that post Lincoln strongly desired to name Joseph Holt, who had served with distinction as war secretary in the latter days of the Buchanan administration.[1] But Holt was too conservative for the Radicals, whose support Lincoln regarded as vital. When the president asked Cameron's opinion about his successor, he mentioned Stanton, a celebrated lawyer who as attorney general had helped stiffen Buchanan's backbone during the secession crisis.[2]

Seven years earlier, Stanton had humiliated Lincoln when they worked together on a major trial involving the McCormick Reaper Company, which brought suit against the John H. Manny Company of Rockford, Illinois.[3] Because the case was originally scheduled to be tried in Illinois before Judge Thomas Drummond, Manny hired Lincoln as associate counsel, paying him a retainer of one thousand dollars in order to keep McCormick from employing him.[4] The lead attorney for Manny, George Harding of Philadelphia, said that Lincoln's name was suggested because he knew Judge Drummond and because the firm wanted to have local talent on the legal team. Harding, who wished to hire Edwin M. Stanton of Pittsburgh as his partner in the case, was unenthusiastic about Lincoln. Reluctantly he dispatched an associate, Peter H. Watson, to consult with the Springfield attorney. When Watson knocked on the door of the house at Eighth and Jackson Streets, Mary Lincoln poked her head out of a window and asked, "Who is there?"

Watson explained that he had come from Philadelphia to see her husband.

"Business or politics?" she queried.

"When told it was business, she (Mrs. Lincoln) indicated her satisfaction by the modified tone in which she shouted, 'Abe, there is a man wants to see you on business.'"

Dressed casually, Lincoln opened the door and invited Watson into the parlor, which his guest found unprepossessing. As Harding later recalled, "Watson was satisfied that he was not the associate we wanted, but, after some conversation, concluded that Lincoln had qualities which might be rather effective in that community, that it would be unwise to incur his hostility by turning him down after consulting him, and paid him a retainer (at which he seemed much surprised), arranged for quite a substantial fee to be paid at the close of the litigation, and left him under the impression that he was to make an argument and should prepare himself for it."

When Watson reported back to Harding, they agreed that Lincoln would not in fact help present the argument but that Stanton would be hired to do so and that Lincoln would be sidetracked. They did not inform the Springfield lawyer of this alteration in plans. When the trial was moved from Chicago to Cincinnati, to suit the convenience of Justice John McLean, who was to preside instead of Drummond, the need for Lincoln's services as "local talent" disappeared. Instead of letting him go, Harding and Watson allowed him to proceed writing his brief.[5] Those two sophisticated gentlemen were taken aback when they first beheld their co-counsel, "a tall, rawly boned, ungainly back woodsman, with coarse, ill-fitting clothes, his trousers hardly reaching his ankles, holding

in his hands a blue cotton umbrella with a ball on the end of the handle."
After being introduced, Lincoln suggested that they proceed to the court
"in a gang." Stanton drew Harding aside and said, "Let that fellow go
with his gang. We'll walk up together." And so they did, snubbing Lincoln. At the courthouse, Stanton emphatically announced that only he
and Harding would be arguing their client's case. Harding recalled that
Stanton "managed to make it plain to Lincoln that we expected him
to withdraw, and, upon his offering to do so, he was taken at his word
instantly, and treated as no longer connected with the case."[6]

Throughout the trial, Harding and Stanton continued to snub Lincoln. When he asked Watson to present Harding a copy of the argument he had laboriously prepared, the Philadelphia attorney returned
it unopened. Ralph Emerson, an officer of the Manny Company who
had suggested that Lincoln be hired, said that the Springfield attorney
"felt that he had been 'tricked' out of the case & the transaction deeply
affected him. He said McLean was not friendly to him & he felt he had
been shabbily treated all around."[7] (McLean had not invited him to a
dinner where the other counselors were guests.)[8] Emerson recalled that
"when it was decided that he should not take part in the argument, he
invited me to his room to express his bitter disappointment, and it was
with difficulty that I persuaded him to remain as counsel during the
hearing."[9] Watson also urged him to stay on. (According to Mrs. Manny,
"it required no little management on the part of Watson to reconcile
Lincoln to the situation.")[10] Stanton referred to Lincoln as a "giraffe"
and a "long-armed baboon."[11] Harding said that "in all his experience
he had never seen one man insult another more grossly, and that too
without reason, than Stanton insulted Lincoln on that occasion." Stanton
"conducted himself toward Lincoln in such a way that it was evident that
he, Stanton, thought Lincoln was of no importance, and deserved no
consideration whatever from himself, and he refused to talk with him,
and told Harding that it was shameful that such a low-down country
lawyer should be sent to associate with them." Stanton "refused to walk

with Lincoln or to be seen on the street with him." In court, Stanton "refused to talk with, or say anything to Lincoln, but utterly ignored him, even refusing to take from Lincoln's hands one of the models used in the case."[12]

Stanton once rudely jerked Lincoln by the coattails and told him to step aside as lawyers examined the reapers on display.[13] Thereafter, Stanton "did not attempt to conceal his unkind feelings" toward Lincoln. According to William Martin Dickson, at whose home Lincoln stayed, his houseguest "was deeply grieved and mortified." All during the trial, as he sat on the sidelines while Stanton argued the case, Lincoln "seemed to be greatly depressed, and gave evidence of that tendency to melancholy which so marked his character." As he left town, Lincoln told his hostess, "You have made my stay here most agreeable, and I am a thousand times obliged to you; but in reply to your request for me to come again I must say to you I never expect to be in Cincinnati again. I have nothing against the city, but things have so happened here as to make it undesirable for me ever to return here."[14]

Seven years later, as Lincoln was considering Cameron's replacement, he consulted with Harding. Asked his opinion about a new war secretary, Harding replied, "I have in mind only one man, but I know you could not and would not appoint him after the outrageous way he has insulted you and behaved towards you in the Reaper case."

"Oh," replied Lincoln, "you mean Stanton. Now, Mr. Harding, this is not a personal matter. I simply desire to do what will be the best thing for the country."[15]

Later Stanton ruefully said, "What a mistake I made about that man when I met him in Cincinnati."[16]

In choosing Cameron's replacement, Lincoln showed political savvy as well as magnanimity. Stanton was politically attractive, for, like Cameron, he lived in Pennsylvania and had been a Democrat. In addition, his service in President James Buchanan's cabinet had made him famous as a staunch Unionist. Lincoln decided to pass over other candidates for the war department portfolio, including Holt, Montgomery Blair, John A. Dix, and Benjamin F. Wade, and name Stanton.

At Lincoln's invitation, Stanton visited the White House with Harding, who recalled that the president and his secretary of war–designate greeted each other with little embarrassment. "The meeting was brief but friendly and Lincoln and Stanton shook hands cordially at parting, both thanking him [Harding] for the trouble he had taken in bringing them together."[17]

Before announcing Stanton's appointment, Lincoln asked Congressman Henry L. Dawes, who served on a committee investigating government transactions during the secession crisis, "whether any thing appeared in that investigation reflecting on the integrity" of Stanton. The president explained that he did not doubt Stanton's integrity, but "it is necessary that the public as well as I should have confidence in the man I appoint to office, whatever may be my own opinion." Later, when Dawes congratulated Lincoln on his choice, he replied "that it was an experiment which he had made up his mind to try, and that whenever a Union man was willing to break away from party affiliations, and stand by the government in this great struggle, he was resolved to give him an opportunity and welcome him to the service." He added "that he had been warned against this appointment, and had been told that it never would do; that 'Stanton would run away with the whole concern, and that he would find he could do nothing with such a man unless he let him have his own way.'" Lincoln "then told a story of a minister out in Illinois who was in the habit of going off on such high flights at camp meetings that they had to put bricks in his pockets to keep him down. 'I may have to do that with Stanton; but if I do, bricks in his pocket will be better than bricks in his hat. I guess I'll let him jump a while.'"[18] To a delegation from Boston and Philadelphia, the president said that he knew Stanton "to be a true and loyal man, and that he possessed the greatest energy of character and systematic method in the discharge of public business."[19]

The new secretary cut an unimpressive figure. According to General John Pope, Stanton

> was in no sense an imposing person, either in looks or manner. He was below the medium stature, stout and clumsy. He had a broad, rather red face, well covered with a heavy black beard, which descended on his breast and was scarcely sprinkled with gray. He had a mass of long hair, pushed off toward the back of his head from a broad, massive brow and large, dark eyes, which looked even larger behind a pair of gold-rimmed spectacles, seemingly of unusual size. His rather squat figure, surmounted by the Iconine bust and head above it, gave him a shaggy, belligerent sort of look, which, to say the least, was not encouraging to the man in search of favors. His speech was quick and apparently positive.[20]

Former California senator William M. Gwin, who had known Stanton years before, predicted that the new war secretary "will tomahawk them all."[21] But most observers approved of the choice, among them George Templeton Strong of the U.S. Sanitary Commission, who thought that at the very least, Stanton was worth "a wagon load of Camerons," for he was prompt, intelligent, earnest, and warm-hearted. Though Strong did not admire Stanton's "rather pigfaced," "Luther-oid" appearance, the new war secretary represented "the reverse in all things of his cunning, cold-blooded, selfish old predecessor."[22] An astute Washington correspondent called Stanton "a very able man, a pushing, all-alive man."[23] The conservative New York *Herald* predicted that "what Carnot was to the first French republic, as Minister of War, Stanton will be to 'Honest Abe Lincoln'; that he will be the man to bring order out of confusion, efficiency out of inaction, and an invincible army out of raw recruits, dispirited by frequent disasters, delays and disappointments."[24]

Lincoln's preferred candidate for the war portfolio, Joseph Holt, thanked the president for choosing Stanton: "In him you will find a friend true as steel, & a support, which no pressure from within or from without, will ever shake. It was my fortune to know him during the darkest days of the late administration & I think I know him well. With his great talents, he is the soul of honor, of courage, & of loyalty. In the progress of the terrible events inseparable from the struggle for the life of our country, in which you are heroically engaged, you can assign to Edwin M. Stanton no duty however stern, or solemn or self-sacrificing, which he will not nobly & efficiently perform."[25] Edwards Pierrepont described to Lincoln "the reviving confidence which your appointment of Mr Stanton had given us. The whole nation thanks God, that you had the wisdom and the courage to make the change."[26] The Democratic mayor of New York praised Lincoln extravagantly: "Your highly patriotic, and conservative course meets with the hearty concurrence of the Democratic masses in this state—We will sustain you fully, and you may rely upon my best exertions in behalf of the administration of which you are the noble head—The late change in the cabinet was opportune—It has given the best proof of your own ability to govern, and also of your executive power and will."[27]

When some Republicans protested against the appointment of a prominent Democrat as secretary of war, Lincoln told them, "If I could find four more democrats just like Stanton, I would appoint them."[28] He said "he knew him to be a true and loyal man, and that he possessed the greatest energy of character and systematic method in the discharge of public business."[29] Democrats were gratified. "The President in [choosing] Mr. Stanton shows that he means to administer the Government, not alone upon a narrow Chicago Platform, but upon the Constitutional National Platform," New York editor James Brooks declared.[30]

In the New York *Tribune*, Charles A. Dana lauded his good friend Stanton as a man who cared deeply about the preservation of the Union. "If slavery or anti-slavery shall at any time be found obstructing or impeding the nation in its efforts to crush out this monstrous rebellion, he will walk straight on the path of duty, though that path should lead him over or through the impediment, and insure its annihilation." The energetic Stanton would infuse energy into the war department, Dana predicted, and would be a "zealous cooperator" rather than "a lordly superior" in dealing with McClellan.[31]

Thanking Dana, Stanton expressed the hope that all Unionists would support him. "Bad passions, and little passions, and mean passions gather around and hem in the great movements that should deliver this nation," he said. But he sensed a new determination in his department. "We have no jokes or trivialities," he assured Dana, "but all with whom I act show that they are now in dead earnest. . . . As soon as I can get the machinery of the office working, the rats cleaned out, & the ratholes stopped, we shall *move.*"[32]

Joseph Medill of the Chicago *Tribune* spoke for many Northerners when he told Stanton that the "country looks to you to infuse vigor, system, honesty, and *fight* into the services. The army has lost more men in the past four months from inaction and ennui than it would have done from ten bloody battles."[33] In the *Missouri Democrat*, John Hay described Stanton as "an energetic and efficient worker, a man of initiative and decision, an organizer, a man of administrative scope and executive tact" who "is personally friendly" with all the members of the cabinet.[34]

Hay reckoned without Montgomery Blair, who had earlier expressed doubt about Stanton's integrity.[35] Bates also distrusted Stanton, and Gideon Welles complained that Stanton's "remarks on the personal appearance of the President were coarse, and his freely expressed judgment on public measures unjust." The navy secretary believed Stanton "was engaged with discontented and mischievous persons in petty intrigues to impair confidence in the Administration."[36] (Indeed, Stanton had criticized Lincoln severely in private, and the Washington rumor mill spread his caustic comments far and wide. McClellan recalled the "extreme virulence with which he abused the President, the administration, and the Republican party. He carried this to such an extent that I was often shocked by it. He never spoke of the President in any other way than as the 'original gorilla.'")[37] Welles also objected to the way Stanton curried McClellan's favor.[38]

Despite those unfortunate qualities, Stanton proved to be a remarkably capable war secretary who worked well with the president. Whereas the selection of his first secretary of war was one of Lincoln's greatest mistakes, the choice of a successor turned out to be one of his most inspired appointments. Shortly after Stanton took over the helm of the war department, Joshua Speed praised the way he transformed it: "Instead of that loose shackeling way of doing business in the war office, with which I have been so much disgusted & which I have had so good an opportunity of seeing, there is now order, regularity and precision. . . . I shall be much mistaken if he does not infuse into the whole army an energy & activity which we have not seen heretofore."[39]

Unlike the president, Stanton had little trouble saying "no." Early in his tenure at the war department, the new secretary was approached by a man who wanted an army appointment and said he had received Lincoln's endorsement. "The President, sir, is a very excellent man and would be glad if he had an appointment for every man who applied, which, unfortunately for his good nature, is not the case," Stanton explained.[40] Later, when a California judge asked for a pass to visit his brother in Virginia, Lincoln suggested he see Stanton. The judge replied that he had done so and was refused. With a smile Lincoln observed, "I can do nothing; for you must know that I have very little influence with this administration."[41] Stanton thus helped the president seem accommodating by assuming the unpleasant but necessary duty of denying requests. His gruffness was useful, for, as General Pope observed, no one "can compute what was the value to the government, of this terse, not to say abrupt treatment of men and business by the Secretary of War in the times when Mr. Stanton held that office. No politician nor suave man of any description could have disposed of such a mass of business and such a crowd of people as pressed on the Secretary of War from morning until night and until far into the early hours of the next day, for months together."[42]

Three months after Lincoln's assassination, John Hay told Stanton that "[n]ot everyone knows, as I do, how close you stood to our lost leader, how he loved you and trusted you, and how vain were all the efforts to shake that trust and confidence, not lightly given & never withdrawn."[43]

The following excerpt is from Nicolay and Hay, *Abraham Lincoln: A History*, 6:139–147:

The relation of Mr. Lincoln to the members of his Cabinet was one of unusual frankness and cordiality. The President was gifted by nature with a courtesy far excelling the conventionalities of an acquired politeness. With a delicacy which has rarely been equaled, he respected not merely their official authority but also their sentiments, their judgments, their manhood. Though differing widely from him in personal qualities, they returned his courtesy and kindness as a rule with warm friendship, and none of them more sincerely than Mr. Stanton. The President found support in the outspoken counsel and robust energy of his war minister; the Secretary yielded trustfully to the superior sagacity and authority of the President. Lincoln began by giving his new Secretary that full discretion which his selection properly implied, and which the vast and responsible duties expected of him unavoidably demanded. It may safely be asserted that Stanton employed this trust with high patriotic aspiration. In comparison with the general correctness of his judgment and the value of his advice and action, his few mistakes which might be pointed out become trivial. The occasional exhibitions of temper and brusqueness of manner which have been observed in him, are chargeable to the harassing perplexity of his duties; naturally he was genial and kind, and his words often evinced a deep tenderness of feeling. As he did not spare his own health and strength in the public service by day or by night, so he required from every subordinate, whether a general or a private, whether in Washington or in the farthest camp, unremitting activity, devotion, sacrifice. Both the War Department and the army instantly felt the quickening influence of his rare organizing power, combined with a will which nothing but unquestioning obedience would satisfy. He insisted rigidly upon military system, discipline, and duty. There was indeed urgent need for their enforcement. The hundreds of thousands of civilians suddenly called to arms as soldiers or officers did not take kindly to the subordination and restraints of the camp. The flood of promotions which attended the organization of brigades and divisions produced an unhealthy rivalry in all grades of command, showering Congress, the War Department, and the Executive Mansion with applications. The evil of officers' furloughs to come to Washington to further their promotions became so great as to excite the wit of the newspapers. "The other day," ran a paragraph, "a boy threw a stone at a dog on Pennsylvania Avenue and hit three Brigadier Generals."

Stanton took hold of such abuses with an energetic hand. He banished self-seeking "shoulder-straps" from the capital. He centered the telegraph in the War Department, where the publication of military news, which might prematurely reach the enemy, could be supervised, and, if necessary, delayed. He expanded and vivified his various military bureaus. He found some Congressmen, like some contractors, misrepresenting his peremptory refusals of the special favors they arrogantly demanded; to correct this abuse, he for a period stood every day at a stated hour beside a tall desk in one of the rooms of the War Department, where he compelled each applicant or interviewer, high or low, to state his request publicly and audibly in presence of the assembled throng, so that the stenographer at his elbow could record it as well as the Secretary's answer, and verbal solicitations and personal interviews diminished suddenly under this staring publicity. It was Stanton's habit to go personally with news or official papers to the Executive Mansion, informally, at all hours; it was Lincoln's practice to go as informally to Stanton's office at the War Department, and in times of great suspense, during impending or actual battles, to spend hour after hour with his War Secretary, where he could read the telegrams as fast as they were received and handed in from the adjoining room. Under such conditions there grew up between them an intimacy in which the mind and heart of each were given without reserve to the great work in which they bore such conspicuous parts. When the time for Mr. Lincoln's reelection came, no man desired or labored for it more earnestly than Edwin M. Stanton, while no one appreciated more clearly or valued more highly than President Lincoln the splendid abilities and services of his Secretary of War.

The anecdotes of his occasional blunt disregard of the President's expressed wishes are either untrue or are half-truths that lead to erroneous conclusions, and originated probably in a certain roughness of Stanton's manner under strong irritation. Lincoln never magnified trifles; Stanton seldom neglected a plain duty. Nevertheless, in the multifarious details of their daily labors they sometimes found each other at cross-purpose in regard to some minor and relatively unimportant matter. Stanton, carrying out the great operations of the War Department, in which system and order were essential, was predisposed to insist upon adherence to established rules. Lincoln, on the other hand, governing the greater machine of administration, which included the temper and drift of public opinion equally with the rules and articles of war, was by nature as well as by reason constantly moved, not merely to the pardoning power with which he was specially invested by the Constitution, but also to that unwritten dispensing authority enfolded within the broad scope of Executive discretion, and was prone to temper the harsh accidents of civil war by a generous and liberal construction of law and duty. It is quite possible that Stanton thought the President too ready to yield to the hundreds of personal petitions which besieged him for clemency or relief, and we have the written evidence that in the following case at least (though we believe the authentic instances are rare), the President's written direction was neglected by his Secretary until reminded of his proper duty by this note from Mr. Lincoln. "A poor widow, by the name of Baird, has a son in the army, that for some offense has been sentenced to serve a long time without pay, or at most with very little pay. I do not like this punishment of withholding pay—it falls so very hard upon poor families.

After he had been serving in this way for several months, at the tearful appeal of the poor mother, I made a direction that he be allowed to enlist for a new term, on the same conditions as others. She now comes, and says she cannot get it acted upon. Please do it." Stanton had his warm-hearted as well as his hot-tempered and stubborn moods, and it is not likely, after this patient explanation, that he hesitated an instant to carry out the President's request. The strong will of Stanton met in Lincoln a still stronger personality, which governed not merely by higher legal authority, but by the manifestation of a greater soul and a clearer insight justifying his decisions with a convincing logic. To show how effectively and yet how prudently the President wielded this weapon, we quote another letter written by him upon a kindred class of topics:

> I am so pressed in regard to prisoners of war in our custody, whose homes are within our lines and who wish to not be exchanged, but to take the oath and be discharged, that I hope you will pardon me for again calling up the subject. My impression is that we will not ever force the exchange of any of this class; that, taking the oath and being discharged, none of them will again go to the rebellion; but the rebellion again coming to them, a considerable percentage of them, probably not a majority, would rejoin it; that by a cautious discrimination, the number so discharged would not be large enough to do any considerable mischief in any event, would relieve distress in at least some meritorious cases, and would give me some relief from an intolerable pressure. I shall be glad, therefore, to have your cheerful assent to the discharge of those whose names I may send, which I will only do with circumspection.

In answer to the above letter, Stanton, on the next day, wrote: "Mr. President: Your order for the discharge of any prisoners of war will be cheerfully and promptly obeyed."

As Lincoln thus always treated Stanton, not as a department clerk, but with the respect and consideration due a Cabinet minister, questions of difference rarely came to a head. There were very few instances in which they ever became sufficiently defined to leave a written record. One such was when the President ordered Franklin's division to join McClellan, against Stanton's desire that it should be kept with McDowell's army moving by land to cover Washington. Another when Stanton with several other members of the Cabinet signed a protest against McClellan's being placed in command of the Army of the Potomac after Pope's defeat in Virginia. In this instance these Cabinet signers had the good sense not to send their protest to Mr. Lincoln. Still a third when Stanton made an order giving Bishop [Edward R.] Ames control of the Methodist churches which had fallen into our hands in the South, in plain violation of a prior letter from the President that the Government must not "undertake to run the churches." In these and similar cases Stanton yielded readily. One authentic case remains where the trial of will between the two men was brought to the point of a sharper issue. It is related by General James B. Fry, who witnessed the scene. Its beginning is sufficiently stated in the following order, made by Lincoln on September 1, 1864:

> It is represented to me that there are at Rock Island, Illinois, as rebel prisoners of war, many persons of Northern and foreign birth who are unwilling to be exchanged and sent South, but who wish to take the oath of allegiance and enter the military service of the Union. Colonel Huidekoper, on behalf of the people of some parts of Pennsylvania, wishes to pay the bounties the Government would have to pay to proper persons of this class, have them enter the service of the United States, and be credited to the localities furnishing the bounty money. He will therefore proceed to Rock Island, ascertain the names of such persons (not including any who have attractions Southward), and telegraph them to the Provost-Marshal-General here, whereupon direction will be given to discharge the persons named upon their taking the oath of allegiance; and upon the official evidence being furnished that they shall have been duly received and mustered into the service of the United States, their number will be credited as may be directed by Colonel Huidekoper.

From what followed we may be certain that the President did not understand the full scope and effect of the order, and when Stanton learned all the circumstances he refused to carry it out, and upon Lincoln's reiterating it, refused a second time. General Fry, who was the provost-marshal-general having special charge of such questions, thus continues his narrative:

Then Lincoln went in person to Stanton's office, and I was called there by the latter to state the facts in the case. I reported to the two high officials, as I had previously done to the Secretary alone, that these men already belonged to the United States, being prisoners of war; that they could not be used against the Confederates; that they had no relation whatever to the county to which it was proposed they should be credited; that all that was necessary towards enlisting them in our army for Indian service was the Government's release of them as prisoners of war; that to give them bounty and credit them to a county which owed some of its own men for service against the Confederates would waste money and deprive the army operating against a powerful enemy of that number of men, etc. Stanton said: "Now, Mr. President, those are the facts, and you must see that your order cannot be executed." Lincoln sat upon a sofa with his legs crossed, and did not say a word until the Secretary's last remark. Then he said, in a somewhat positive tone: "Mr. Secretary, I reckon you'll have to execute the order." Stanton replied with asperity: "Mr. President, I cannot do it. The order is an improper one, and I cannot execute it." Lincoln fixed his eye upon Stanton, and in a firm voice, and with an accent that clearly showed his determination, he said: "Mr. Secretary, it will have to be done." Stanton then realized that he was overmatched. He had made a square issue with the President and been defeated, notwithstanding the fact that he was in the right. Upon an intimation from him I withdrew and did not witness his surrender. A few minutes after I reached my office I received instructions from the Secretary to carry out the President's order.

It must not be assumed from the termination of the above incident that Mr. Lincoln wished either to humiliate the Secretary of War or compel him to violate his convictions of duty. In the interim between General Fry's withdrawal from the room and the Secretary's acquiescence Lincoln had doubtless explained to Stanton, with that irresistible frankness and kindness with which he carried all his points of controversy, the reasons for his insistence, which he immediately further put upon record for the Secretary's justification in the following letter to General Grant, dated September 22, 1864:

> I send this as an explanation to you, and to do justice to the Secretary of War. I was induced, upon pressing applications, to authorize agents of one of the districts of Pennsylvania to recruit in one of the prison depots in Illinois; and the thing went so far before it came to the knowledge of the Secretary that, in my judgment, it could not be abandoned without greater evil than would follow its going through. I did not know at the time that you had protested against that class of thing being done; and I now say that while this particular job must be completed, no other of the sort will be authorized, without an understanding with you, if at all. The Secretary of War is wholly free of any part in this blunder.

8

LINCOLN AND GENERAL GEORGE B. MCCLELLAN

Another striking example of Lincoln's magnanimity was his treatment of General George B. McClellan, who commanded the Army of the Potomac from August 1861 to November 1862. The Young Napoleon, as he was called, snubbed the president on numerous occasions. To his wife, McClellan described Lincoln as "an idiot," "the original gorilla," a "baboon," and "'an old stick'—& pretty poor timber at that." He denounced "the cowardice of the Presdt" and declared that "I can never regard him with feeling other than those of thorough contempt—for his mind, heart & morality."[1]

McClellan manifested his contempt for Lincoln in deeds as well as words. Shortly after his elevation to the supreme command of all Union armies in the fall of 1861, the Young Napoleon returned home from a wedding to discover the president, John Hay, and Secretary of State William Henry Seward waiting for him. According to Hay, the general, "without paying any particular attention to the porter who told him the President was waiting to see him, went up stairs, passing the door of the room where the President and Secretary of State were seated. They waited about half-an-hour, and sent once more a servant to tell the General they were there, and the answer came that the General had done to bed." As they returned to the White House, Hay mentioned "this unparalleled insolence of epaulettes," but Lincoln "seemed not to have noticed it specially, saying it was better at this time not to be making points of etiquette & personal dignity."[2]

This snub was not unprecedented. A month earlier, the English journalist William Howard Russell noted in his diary, "Calling on the General [McClellan] the other night at his usual time of return, I was told by the orderly, who was closing the door, 'The General's gone to bed tired, and can see no one. He sent the same message to the President, who came inquiring after him ten minutes ago.'"[3] Around that same time, Lincoln called at the general's headquarters, only to be told that "he's lying down, very much fatigued."[4] On another occasion, McClellan did not deign to interrupt his breakfast when the president called; Lincoln was kept waiting till the general finished eating, much to the surprise of an observer.[5]

David D. Porter was astounded when a conversation he was having with Little Mac concerning the New Orleans campaign was interrupted by a servant announcing that the president wished to see the general.

"Let him wait," said McClellan. "I am busy."

"Oh," remarked Porter, "don't send such a message to the President, he is very much interested in this matter, and it is not respectful to keep him waiting. Remember that he is our Commander-in-chief."

"Well," said the Young Napoleon, "let the Commander-in-chief wait, he has no business to know what is going on."[6]

In 1862, Lincoln once again found the Young Napoleon unwilling to get out of bed to meet with him. According to one of McClellan's aides, the president called at the general's house one Sunday morning in September and asked to see him. A short while later, McClellan's chief of staff, General Randolph Marcy, "came down and with flushed face and confused manner said he was very sorry but McClellan was not yet up. A strange expression came over Lincoln's face, as he rose and said, 'Of course he's very busy now, and no doubt was laboring far into the night.' He departed hastily."[7] A similar act of rudeness occurred when McClellan failed to keep an appointment with the president, General

Ormsby M. Mitchel, and Ohio Governor William Dennison. After a long wait, Lincoln said with customary forbearance, "Never mind; I will hold McClellan's horse if he will only bring us success."[8] William O. Stoddard recalled how mortified he felt when he accompanied Lincoln to the home of McClellan, who kept the president waiting for an unconscionably long time.[9]

In early 1862, McClellan stood up not only Lincoln but the entire cabinet. As the president told General Ambrose E. Burnside in February, Little Mac "is a good fellow and means well" but he "don't know so much about etiquette as I do. I asked him to come and meet the Cabinet in Consultation the other day and he promised to do so. I called them together at 12 and all came, but no McClellan. At ½ past 12 Seward got impatient and went away, and at one all were gone. At half-past one McClellan came, and when I asked him why he was not here, he said he forgot it." This absent-mindedness reminded Lincoln of one of his legal cases.

> When I was practicing law in Illinois a bad fellow in our town was charged with moral delinquency or in other words rape. He was accused of having committed two outrages on the woman—one in the afternoon and the other next day; everybody believed him guilty and when he applied to me to defend him, I refused; but he plead so hard and assured me so positively that the woman was a willing party that I consented to defend him and took up his cause. My friends remonstrated; but I was so convinced of the man's innocence that I determined to go on. At the trial, the woman gave . . . excellent direct testimony. I saw its effect on the jury and that it must be overcome; & in the cross examination I led her off to other topics and then suddenly returned to the charge.
>
> "Did you sleep with your husband after the first outrage?"
> "She said 'Yes.'"
> "Did you tell him about it?"
> "No—I forgot."[10]

Even when Little Mac did allow the president to consult with him, he would not say much. In mid-December 1861, George Bancroft accompanied Lincoln to McClellan's house. Bancroft described the Young Napoleon unflatteringly: "Of all the silent, uncommunicative, reserved men, whom I ever met, the general stands among the first."[11]

Little Mac's contemptuous attitude toward the president was partially rooted in snobbery. The scion of a refined Philadelphia family, McClellan regarded many people as his social inferiors, among them Lincoln. Years after the war, he wrote that the sixteenth president "was not a man of very strong character, & as he was destitute of refinement—certainly in no sense a gentleman—he was easily wrought upon by coarse associates whose style of conversation agreed so well with his own."[12]

In late June 1862, as McClellan was driven back from Richmond by Robert E. Lee's bold attacks, he sent an astounding telegram from Savage Station to Stanton.

If we have lost the day we have yet preserved our honor & no one need blush for the Army of the Potomac. I have lost this battle because my force was too small. I again repeat that I am not responsible for this & I say it with the earnestness of a General who feels in his heart the loss of every brave man who has been needlessly sacrificed today. I still hope to retrieve our fortunes, but to do this the Govt must view the matter in the same earnest light that I do—you must send me very large reinforcements, & send them at once. I shall draw back to this side of Chickahominy & think I can withdraw all our material. Please understand that in this battle we have lost nothing but men & those the best we have. In addition to what I have already said I only wish to say to the Presdt that I think he is wrong, in regarding me as ungenerous when I said that my force was too weak. I merely intimated a truth which today has been too plainly proved. I should have gained this battle with (10,000) ten thousand fresh men. If at this instant I could dispose of (10,000) ten thousand fresh men I could gain a victory tomorrow. I know that a few thousand more men would have changed this battle from a defeat to a victory—as it is the Govt must not & cannot hold me responsible for the result. I feel too earnestly to-night—I have seen too many dead & wounded comrades to feel otherwise than that the Govt has not sustained this Army. If you do not do so now the game is lost. If I save this army now I tell you plainly that I owe no thanks to you or any other persons in Washington—you have done your best to sacrifice this Army.[13]

Before passing this insubordinate message on to his boss, the scandalized supervisor of telegraphs in the war department, Edward S. Sanford, omitted the last sentence. Even in its bowdlerized version, that telegram angered Stanton, who took it to Lincoln and said "with much feeling 'You know—Mr President that all I have done was by your authority.'"[14]

A few days later, Lincoln visited McClellan's army at Harrison's Landing, where the general handed him a long letter urging him to pursue a conservative policy on slavery.

In late August, Lincoln despaired when the Army of Virginia under John Pope lost badly to Lee at Second Bull Run. Even though Lincoln blamed Pope's defeat on McClellan's failure to support him, the president reappointed Little Mac to command the army over the fierce objections of some of the cabinet. When Lee invaded Maryland in September, McClellan fought him to a draw at the battle of Antietam, after which Lee retreated back across the Potomac.

The following excerpt is from Nicolay and Hay, *Abraham Lincoln: A History* 6:22–29:

Mr. Lincoln certainly had the defects of his great qualities. His unbounded magnanimity made him sometimes incapable even of just resentments. General McClellan's worst offenses had been committed against the President in person. The insulting dispatch from Savage's Station and the letter from Harrison's Landing, in which he took the President to task for the whole course of his civil and military administration, would probably have been pardoned by no other ruler that ever lived; yet Mr. Lincoln never appeared to bear the slightest ill-will to the general on account of these affronts. He did feel deeply the conduct of McClellan towards Pope. He was outraged at McClellan's suggestion to leave Pope to his fate. He said to one of his household [John Hay] on the 30th of August, "He has acted badly towards Pope; he really wanted him to fail"; and after he had placed him again in command of the Army of the Potomac he repeated this severe judgment, but he added, "There is no one in the army who can man these fortifications and lick these troops of ours into shape half as well as he can." Again he said, "We must use the tools we have; if he cannot fight himself, he excels in making others ready to fight." In the interests of the country he condoned the offenses against Pope as readily as those against himself.

It may perhaps even be said that McClellan, so far from suffering at the President's hands for his unbecoming conduct towards him, gained a positive advantage by it. It was not alone for his undoubted talents as an organizer and drill-master that he was restored to his command. It was a time of gloom and doubt in the political as well as in the military situation. The factious spirit was stronger among the politicians and the press of the Democratic party than at any other time during the war. Not only in the States of the border, but in many Northern States, there were signs of sullen discontent among a large body of the people that could not escape the notice of a statesman so vigilant as Lincoln. It was of the greatest importance, not only in the interest of recruiting, but also in the interest of that wider support which a popular Government requires from the general body of its citizens, that causes of offense against any large portion of the community should be sedulously avoided by those in power. General McClellan had made himself, by his demonstration against the President's policy, the leader of the Democratic party. Mr. Lincoln, for these reasons, was especially anxious to take no action against McClellan which might seem to be dictated by personal jealousy or pique; and besides, as General Pope had himself reported, there was a personal devotion to McClellan among those in high command in the Army of the Potomac which rendered it almost impossible for any other general to get its best work out of it. General Ethan Allen Hitchcock, one of the most accomplished officers of the old army, gave this as the reason for his declining that command.

It is difficult to regard without indignation the treatment, however necessary and justifiable, which the principal actors in this great transaction received. McClellan, whose conduct from beginning to end can only be condemned, received the command of a great army, reorganized and reenforced, and with it a chance for magnificent achievement, if he had been able to improve it, which no officer before or since ever enjoyed on this continent. Pope, who had fought with the greatest bravery and perseverance a losing battle against Lee's entire army all the way from the Rapidan to the Potomac, encouraged at every point with the hope of reenforcements which only reached him too late, and finally by his misfortune adding a new luster to the prestige of his rival and enemy, received simply the compliments and congratulations of his superiors and was then removed to a distant department of the frontier, to take no further part in the stirring scenes of a war in which he was so well qualified to bear an honorable part. McDowell, a perfect soldier, among the bravest, ablest, and most loyal officers of the army, who had done his whole duty and much more, who zealously went before and beyond the orders of his superiors, always seeking the post of utmost danger and toil, was found at the close of this campaign, in which his conduct deserved the highest credit, with his reputation so smirched and tarnished by calumny that he was never after during the war considered available for those high and important employments for which he was better equipped than almost any of his comrades. A court of inquiry, it is true, vindicated him completely from every charge that malice or ignorance had invented against him; but the two disasters of Bull Run, in successive summers, for neither of which he was to blame, remained in the popular mind inseparably connected with his name.

General McClellan himself never appreciated the magnanimity with which he had been treated. In fact, he thought the magnanimity was all upon his side. As time wore on he continually exaggerated in his own mind the services he had rendered and the needs of the Government at the time he had been placed in command, until he created for himself the fantastic delusion that he had saved the Administration from despair! In the last lines he ever wrote, shortly before his death, he gave this absolutely new and most remarkable account of the visit which Lincoln and Halleck made to him on the 2d of September:

> He [the President] then said that he regarded Washington as lost, and asked me if I would, under the circumstances, as a favor to him, resume command and do the best that could be done. Without one moment's hesitation, and without making any conditions whatever, I at once said that I would accept the command and would stake my life that I would save the city. Both the President and Halleck again asserted that it was impossible to save the city, and I repeated my firm conviction that I could and would save it. They then left, the President verbally placing me in entire command of the city and of the troops falling back upon it from the front.

It is possible that in the lapse of twenty years General McClellan's memory had become so distorted by constant dwelling upon imagined wrongs that he was at last capable of believing this fiction. It was a fancy adopted in the last years of his life. A year after his removal from command he wrote a voluminous report of his entire military history, filling an octavo volume. He was then the acknowledged favorite of the Democratic party, the predestined candidate for the Presidency in opposition to Lincoln. He embodied in that report every incident or argument he could think of to justify his own conduct and to condemn that of the Government. Yet in this long narrative there is no hint that Lincoln or Halleck thought the capital was lost. He apparently never dreamed of such a thing while Lincoln lived; he gave no intimation of such a charge while Halleck survived, although their relations were frankly hostile. Only after both these witnesses had passed away, and a direct contradiction was thus rendered impossible, did it occur to him to report

this conversation between his patriotic heroism and their cra-
ven despair!

There is another proof that this story was an afterthought.
In a letter to his family, written on the 2d, the very morning of
this pretended conversation, he merely says: "I was surprised
this morning, when at breakfast, by a visit from the President
and Halleck, in which the former expressed the opinion that the
troubles now impending could be overcome better by me than
anyone else. Pope is ordered to fall back upon Washington, and as
he reenters everything is to come under my command again."

When we consider that in these private letters he never omits
an opportunity for heroic posturing, it is impossible to believe
that if Lincoln and Halleck an hour or two before had been
imploring him to save the capital, he would not have mentioned
it. The truth is, McClellan himself has left evidence of the fact
that it was he who thought Washington in danger. On the 31st
of August he wrote to his wife: "I do not regard Washington as
safe against the rebels. If I can quietly slip over there I will send
your silver off." If it were worth while to cumber these pages
with the refutation of a calumny so transparently false, we could
bring the testimony of a score of witnesses to show that Mr. Lincoln, during the first days of September, was unusually cool and
determined. Grieved and disappointed as he was at the failure
of Pope's campaign, his principal preoccupation was not at any
time the safety of Washington. It was that Lee's army, as he frequently expressed it, "should not get away without being hurt."
On Monday morning he said: "They must be whipped here and
now. Pope must fight them; and if they are too strong for him,
he can gradually get back to these fortifications." At the time
McClellan represents him as hopeless of saving Washington he
had no thought of the safety of that place in his mind, except
as a secondary and permanent consideration. He was making
ready a force to attack the enemy. On the 3d of September he
wrote with his own hand this order, which sufficiently shows
the mood he was in:

"*Ordered*, that the General-in-Chief, Major-General Halleck, immediately commence and proceed with all possible

dispatch to organize an army for active operations from all the material within and coming within his control, independent of the forces he may deem necessary for the defense of Washington, when such active army shall take the field."

This order, countersigned by the Secretary of War, was delivered to Halleck by General [E. D.] Townsend, and the work of preparing the army for the offensive was at once begun. McClellan, under Halleck's direction, went heartily to work to execute the orders of the President. He had none of the protecting airs he gives himself in his memoirs; his conduct was exemplary. "McClellan," said Lincoln on the 5th, "is working like a beaver. He seems to be aroused to doing something by the sort of snubbing he got last week." The work he was now engaged upon was congenial staff work, and he performed it with great zeal and efficiency. It suited him in after years to pretend that he was acting without orders and without communication with the Government. It was his favorite phrase that he went to Antietam with a "halter about his neck." But his letters written at the time contradict such assertions. He wrote from Washington, on the 7th of September: "I leave here this afternoon to take command of the troops in the field. The feeling of the Government towards me, I am sure, is kind and trusting."

9

REMOVAL OF MCCLELLAN FROM COMMAND:
NOVEMBER 1862

After the battle of Antietam on September 17, 1862, McClellan, fearing that he would be attacked and that his army was too disorganized to move, dawdled in his usual fashion, allowing Lee to escape across the Potomac from Maryland to Virginia. When Little Mac boasted that he had achieved a great victory by driving the Confederates from Union soil, the "hearts of 10 million people sank within them," according to Lincoln.[1] No one's heart sank deeper than the president's. In early October, over the objections of most cabinet members, he visited the Army of the Potomac hoping to goad the general into action.[2]

In addition, Lincoln said he wanted "to satisfy himself personally without the intervention of anybody, of the purposes intentions and fidelity of McClellan, his officers, and the army."[3] Thomas J. Barnett, a Washington insider, reported that the administration had "a dread of the army" and feared "revolution in the North."[4] This anxiety was not irrational. The adjutant general of the Army of the Potomac, Thomas M. Key, stated that "the 'traitor' element near McClellan had constantly grown bolder" and "they daily talked of overthrowing the Government and making McClellan dictator." Key reported that after the preliminary Emancipation Proclamation was announced, "this element felt that McClellan would not long remain in command: that then was the time to move or never—that an appeal could be made to the army setting forth that this proclamation was a usurpation, the conversion of the war for the Union into a John Brown Abolition raid and thus was a subversion of the Constitution absolving the army from its allegiance: that a movement should be made upon Washington to restore the Constitution."[5]

During his three-day stay with the army, Lincoln spoke often with McClellan, who acknowledged that the president "was very kind personally—told me he was convinced I was the best general in the country etc etc. He was very affable & I really think he does feel very kindly towards me personally."[6] Though pleasant in manner, Lincoln was stern in substance, asking tough questions and offering blunt criticism. He was puzzled to see most of the new recruits in Frederick, twenty miles from the veteran army units at Sharpsburg. "Why was this? Why were not green troops and veterans mixed together?" he asked Little Mac.

"We have not tent equipage and cannot well move up the new levies!" came the reply.

"Why are the troops any worse off at Sharpsburg without tents than at Frederick without tents?" the president asked. No satisfactory answer was offered.[7]

Frankly Lincoln warned the general "that he w[oul]d be a ruined man if he did not move forward, move rapidly & effectively."[8] According to the New York journalist George Wilkes, Lincoln also said to McClellan, "I wish to call your attention to a fault in your character—a fault which is the sum of my observations of you, in connection with this war. You merely get yourself ready to do a good thing—no man can do that better—you make all the necessary sacrifices of blood and time, and treasure, to secure a victory, *but whether from timidity, self-distrust, or some other motive inexplicable to me, you always stop short just on this side of results.*"[9] He instructed McClellan to launch an advance within two weeks.[10] Unmoved by Lincoln's criticism, the general wrote his wife about the presidential entourage, "These people don't know what an army requires & therefore act stupidly."[11]

If the Young Napoleon was disgusted with Lincoln, the feeling was mutual. One evening, the president asked Ozias M. Hatch as they stood on a hill surveying the vast encampment, "Hatch, what do you suppose all these people are?"

"Why, I suppose it to be a part of the grand army."

Lincoln, "in a tone of patient but melancholy sarcasm," corrected him: "No, you are mistaken."

"What are they then?"

"That is General McClellan's body guard."[12]

Though Lincoln "expressed himself eminently satisfied with the discipline and appearance of the troops," he was dismayed to learn they numbered only 93,000, though 180,000 were on the muster rolls.[13] He cited similar figures to Admiral Samuel F. P. Du Pont as he bemoaned the "melting away" of the army. "These are the facts," he said; "how they are to be cured *I don't know.*" In part Lincoln seemed to blame the Sanitary Commission (a precursor of the Red Cross), which he called "the sentimental department of the army." The president evidently shared Halleck's view that commission members encouraged the discharge of many soldiers who were not seriously sick or wounded.[14] (In August, Lincoln had lamented to Benjamin Brown French that "although the army consisted nominally of 600,000 men, from the best information that he could get there were not, at that moment, over 362,000 available fighting men in our army.")[15] Some of the officers who should have been in the field infested Washington, availing themselves of brothels and saloons when not lobbying for promotion. "These fellows *and the Congressmen* do vex me sorely!" Lincoln exclaimed.[16]

Shortly after his return to Washington on October 4, Lincoln had Halleck order McClellan to "cross the Potomac and give battle to the enemy or drive him south. Your army must move now while the roads are good."[17] For the next month, Little Mac deluged Washington authorities with justifications for staying put. Among other things, he complained that his men lacked shoes, clothing, and horses.

In response to McClellan's explanation that his horses were exhausted, Lincoln sent a tart reply through Halleck: "The President has read your telegram, and directs me to suggest that, if the enemy had more occupation south of the river, his cavalry would not be so likely to make raids north of it."[18] Shortly thereafter, Lincoln more pointedly wired the Young Napoleon, "I have just received your dispatch about sore tongued and fatiegued [sic] horses. Will you pardon me for asking what the horses of your army have done since the battle of Antietam that fatigue anything?"[19] Indignant at what he considered a "dirty little fling," McClellan sent a lengthy report on his cavalry but failed to deal with Lincoln's larger point, that the army's inactivity threatened the war effort.[20]

Lincoln tried to sooth the general's hurt feelings. "Most certainly I intend no injustice to any; and if I have done any, I deeply regret it. To be told after more than five weeks total inaction of the Army, and during which period we had sent to that Army every fresh horse we possibly could, amounting in the whole to 7918 that the cavalry horses were too much fatigued to move, presented a *very cheerless*, almost hopeless, prospect for the future; and it may have forced something of impatience into my despatches [sic]. If not recruited, and rested then, when could they ever be?"[21]

While McClellan dithered, 1800 Confederate cavalry under Jeb Stuart rode a circle around the Army of the Potomac. Nicolay told his fiancée that Stuart's joyride was "a little thing, accomplishing not much actual harm, and yet infinitely vexatious and mischievous. The President has well-nigh lost his temper over it."[22] With some asperity, Lincoln observed to McClellan that "Stuart's cavalry *outmarched ours*, having certainly done more marked service on the Peninsula, and everywhere since."[23]

On October 13, the president spelled out his central concern to McClellan. "You remember my speaking to you of what I called your over-cautiousness. Are you not over-cautious when you assume that you can not do what the enemy is constantly doing? Should you not claim to be at least his equal in prowess, and act upon the claim?" To McClellan's insistence that he needed to have the rail line from Harper's Ferry repaired before he could move against Lee's army at Winchester, Lincoln replied, "I certainly should be pleased for you to have the advantage of the Railroad from Harper's Ferry to Winchester, but it wastes all the remainder of autumn to give it to you; and, in fact *ignores the question of time*, which can not, and must not be ignored."

Little Mac had expressed fear that while his army moved toward Winchester, the Confederates might attack Pennsylvania. To alleviate this anxiety, Lincoln pointed out that if Lee "does so in full force, he gives up his communications to you absolutely, and you have nothing to do but to follow, and ruin him; if he does so with less than full force, fall upon, and beat what is left behind all the easier." The Army of the Potomac, Lincoln noted, was closer to Richmond than was the Army of Northern Virginia. "Why can you not reach there before him, unless you admit that he is more than your equal on a march. His route is the arc of a circle, while yours is the chord. The roads are as good on yours as on his." If Lee moved toward the Confederate capital, Lincoln suggested that McClellan "press closely to him, fight him if a favorable opportunity should present, and, at least, try to beat him to Richmond on the inside track. I say 'try'; if we never try, we shall never succeed."

Lee might stay put at Winchester, far from Richmond. If he did so, Lincoln urged, the Army of the Potomac should "fight him there, on the idea that if we can not beat him when he bears the wastage of coming to us, we never can when we bear the wastage of going to him. This proposition is a simple truth, and is too important to be lost sight of for a moment. In coming to us, he tenders us an advantage which we should not waive. We should not so operate as to merely drive him away. As we must beat him somewhere, or fail finally, we can do it, if at all, easier near to us, than far away. If we can not beat the enemy where he now is, we never can, he again being within the entrenchments of Richmond." After describing how the Union army could be easily supplied as it moved toward the Confederate capital, Lincoln concluded by saying "This letter is in no sense an order."[24]

Lincoln feared that this long missive would have no effect, even though it implicitly gave McClellan only one last chance to redeem himself. Reluctantly, Little Mac abandoned his own intention to postpone serious action till the spring. Still he dawdled. On October 21, Halleck told him that the president "does not expect impossibilities, but he is very anxious that all this good weather should not be wasted in inactivity."[25]

Five days later, the Young Napoleon finally began marching his army across the Potomac, a process which lasted more than a week. "The President keeps poking sharp sticks under little Mac's ribs, and has screwed up his courage to the point of beginning to cross the river today," Nicolay wrote Hay on October 26.[26] Intemperately, McClellan complained to his wife, "If you could know the mean & dirty character of the dispatches I receive you would boil over with anger—when it is possible to misunderstand, & when it is not possible, whenever there is a chance of a wretched innuendo—there it comes. But the good of the country requires me to submit to all this from men whom I know to be greatly my inferiors socially, intellectually & morally! There never was a truer epithet applied to a certain individual than that of the 'Gorilla.'"[27]

As McClellan moved south at a leisurely pace, Lee swiftly retreated toward Richmond. On November 4, the Confederates were positioned athwart the Young Napoleon's line of advance. Finally out of all patience, Lincoln relieved Little Mac. He had been tempted to do so earlier, but thought it advisable to wait until after the fall elections.[28] He explained that he did not want "to estrange the affections of the Democratic party." He also wished to avoid making the general a martyr.[29] By early November, Nicolay reported, Lincoln's "patience is at last completely exhausted with McClellan's inaction and never-ending excuses." The president "has been exceedingly reluctant to do this. In many respects he thinks McClellan a very superior and efficient officer. This with the high personal regard for him, has led him to indulge him in his whims and complaints and shortcomings as a mother would indulge her baby. He is constitutionally *too slow*, and has fitly been dubbed the great American tortoise."[30] (He was also known as the "Great Do-nothing.")[31]

To Francis P. Blair, Lincoln explained that he "had tried long enough to bore with an auger too dull to take hold." He added, "I said I would remove him if he let Lee's army get away from him, and I must do so. He has got the 'slows,' Mr. Blair." He also told Blair that McClellan's subordinate generals had lost confidence in him.[32] One of those generals, John G. Barnard, said, "If you were to 'count noses' among the officers of the A[rmy of the] P[otomac] whose opinions are worth any thing, I believe you would find that most think and express the opinion that he made the most stupendous failure. He showed himself incapable in the outset of appreciating & grasping his position by utterly failing to do anything—permitting the Potomac to be blockaded in face of his 25000 men—Norfolk to be kept—until he lost the essential requisite to success—*the confidence of the Administration and of the Country.*" Barnard judged that "History records few such opportunities of *greatness offered*—and so *stupendously . . . lost.*"[33]

Lincoln explained to Orville H. Browning that he had "coaxed, urged, and ordered" McClellan to move aggressively, "but all would not do. At the expiration of two weeks after a peremptory order to that effect, he had only three-fourths of his army across the river and was six days doing that, whereas the rebel army had effected a crossing in one day."[34] The president offered a similar account to John Hay:

> After the battle of Antietam, I went up to the field to try to get him to move & came back thinking he would move at once. But when I got home he began to argue why he ought not to move. I peremptorily ordered him to advance. It was 19 days before he put a man over the river. It was 9 days longer before he got his army across and then he stopped again, delaying on little pretexts of wanting this and that. I began to fear he was playing false—that he did not want to hurt the enemy. I saw how he could intercept the enemy on the way to Richmond. I determined to make that the test. If he let them get away I would remove him. He did so & I relieved him.[35]

Lincoln's suspicion that McClellan "did not want to hurt the enemy" was easy to understand, given the general's timidity, but it was unjustified. McClellan desired military success but lacked the boldness to achieve it.[36]

Nicolay and Hay tersely recounted the story of McClellan's dismissal (*Abraham Lincoln: A History*, 6:185–89):

There is no doubt that Mr. Lincoln's regard and confidence, which had withstood so much from General McClellan, was giving way. The President had resisted in his behalf, for more than a year, the earnest and bitter opposition of the most powerful and trusted friends of the Administration. McClellan had hardly a supporter left among the Republican Senators, and few among the most prominent members of the majority in the House of Representatives. In the Cabinet there was the same unanimous hostility to the young general. In the meeting of the 2d of September, when the President announced that he had placed McClellan in command of the forces in Washington, he was met by an outbreak of protest and criticism from the leading members of the Government which might well have shaken the nerves of any ruler. But the President stood manfully by his action. He admitted the infirmities of McClellan, his lack of energy and initiative, but for this exigency he considered him the best man in the service, and the country must have the benefit of his talents, although he had behaved badly. We need not refer again to the magnanimity with which the President had overlooked the insolent dispatches of General McClellan from Savage's Station and Harrison's Bar. He closed his ears persistently during all the months of the winter and spring to the stories which came to him from every quarter in regard to the tone of factious hostility to himself which prevailed at McClellan's headquarters. But these stories increased to such an extent during the summer and autumn that even in his mind, so slow to believe evil, they occasioned some trouble. Soon after the battle of Antietam an incident came to his hearing, of which he felt himself obliged to take notice. Major John J. Key, brother to Colonel Thomas M. Key of McClellan's staff, was reported, replying to a question put by a brother officer, "Why was not the rebel army bagged immediately after the battle near Sharpsburg?" to have said, "That is not the game; the object is that neither army shall get much advantage of the other; that both shall be kept in the field till they are exhausted, when we will make a compromise and save slavery." The President sent a letter to Major Key to inform him of this grave charge, and to invite him to disprove it within twenty-four hours. A few minutes after this notice was sent, the major appeared at the Executive Mansion in company with Major Levi C. Turner, the officer to whom the remark had been made. A trial, as prompt as those of St. Louis dispensing justice under the oak at Vincennes, then took place. The President was judge and jury, attorney for the prosecution and for the defense, and he added to these functions that of clerk of the court, and made a record of the proceedings with his own hand, which we copy from his manuscript:

> At about eleven o'clock A. M., September 27th, 1862, Major Key and Major Turner appear before me. Major Turner says: "As I remember it, the conversation was, I asked the question why we did not bag them after the battle of Sharpsburg. Major Key's reply was, 'That was not the game; that we should tire the rebels out and ourselves; that that was the only way the Union could be preserved; we come together fraternally, and slavery be saved.' On cross-examination Major Turner says he has frequently heard Major Key converse in regard to the present troubles, and never heard him utter a sentiment unfavorable to the maintenance of the Union. He has never uttered anything which he, Major T., would call disloyalty. The particular conversation detailed was a private one.

Upon the reverse of this record the President made the following indorsement: "In my view it is wholly inadmissible for any gentleman holding a military commission from the United States to utter such sentiments as Major Key is within proved to have done. Therefore let Major John J. Key be forthwith dismissed from the military service of the United States."

The President's memorandum continues: "At the interview of Major Key and Major Turner with the President, Major Key did not attempt to controvert the statement of Major Turner, but simply insisted and tried to prove that he was true to the Union. The substance of the President's reply was that if there was a game even among Union men to have our army not take any advantage of the enemy when it could, it was his object to break up that game." Speaking of the matter afterwards the President said, "I dismissed Major Key because I thought his silly, treasonable expressions were 'staff talk' and I wished to make an example."

He was still not ready to condemn General McClellan. He determined to give him one more chance. If McClellan, after Antietam, had destroyed the army of Lee his official position would have been impregnable. If, after Lee had recrossed the Potomac, McClellan had followed and delivered a successful battle in Virginia, nothing could afterwards have prevented his standing as the foremost man of his time. The President, in his intense anxiety for the success of the national arms, would have welcomed McClellan as his own presumptive successor if he could have won that position by successful battle. But the general's inexplicable slowness had at last excited the President's distrust. He began to think, before the end of October, that Mc-Clellan had no real desire to beat the enemy. He set in his own mind the limit of his forbearance. He adopted for his guidance a test which he communicated to no one until long afterwards, on which he determined to base his final judgment of McClel-lan. If he should permit Lee to cross the Blue Ridge and place himself between Richmond and the Army of the Potomac he would remove him from command.

When it was reported in Washington that Lee and Longstreet were at Culpeper Court House, the President sent an order, dated the 5th of November, to General McClellan, which reached him at Rectortown on the 7th, directing him to report for further orders at Trenton, New Jersey, and to turn the command of the

Army of the Potomac over to General [Ambrose E.] Burnside. General C. P. Buckingham delivered his message first to Burnside and then came with him to McClellan's tent. McClellan says in his memoirs that with the eyes of the two generals upon him he "read the papers with a smile"—but when they were gone, he turned to finish a letter he had been writing and broke out in the heartfelt ejaculation, "Alas for my poor country." He took credit to himself in after years for not heading a mutiny of the troops. He said, "Many were in favor of my refusing to obey the order and of marching upon Washington to take possession of the Government."

Thus ended the military career of George Brinton McClellan.

10

CABINET CRISIS: DECEMBER 1862

$\mathcal{I}$n the wake of the disastrous Union defeat at Fredericksburg on December 13, 1862, gloom settled over the people of the North. "They have borne, silently and grimly, imbecility, treachery, failure, privation, loss of friends and means, almost every suffering which can afflict a brave people," observed *Harpers Weekly*. "But they cannot be expected to suffer that such massacres as this at Fredericksburg shall be repeated."[1] Benjamin Brown French gave voice to the widespread pessimism: "Unless something occurs very soon to brighten up affairs, I shall begin to look upon our whole Nation as on its way to destruction."[2]

Lincoln's popularity sank. "A year ago we laughed at the Honest Old Abe's grotesque genial Western jocosities, but they nauseate us now," remarked George Templeton Strong. He predicted that if things continued to go as they had been going, pressure would grow to have Lincoln "resign and make way for Hamlin, as for one about whom nobody knows anything and who may therefore be a change for the better, none for the worse being conceivable."[3] Charles Eliot Norton lamented that while the nation required leadership from "a Bengal tiger," it had only a "domestic cat" in the White House.[4] Constituents told Pennsylvania Representative Edward McPherson that "almost everybody is dissatisfied with the administration. President Lincoln is denounced by many of his most devoted friends in former times." The public was "utterly disgusted," believing "that the present administration is utterly incompetent." Ominously, McPherson was warned that "if things are not more successfully managed the President will be generally deserted."[5] Orestes A. Brownson complained to Charles Sumner, "I do not believe Mr. Lincoln at all. . . . He is thick-headed; he is ignorant; he is tricky, somewhat astute in a small way, and obstinate as a mule."[6] Abolitionist John Jay foresaw a "storm rising that presently will not be stilled by any thing less than an entire reconstruction of the Cabinet."[7] From Boston came a prediction that Lincoln's resignation "would be received with *great satisfaction*" and might "avert what . . . will otherwise come viz a *violent and bloody revolution at the North*."[8]

The president was aware of such threats of violence against him. When told that a Pennsylvanian expressed the hope that Lincoln would be hanged from a lamppost outside the White House, he remarked to Congressman William D. Kelley, "You need not be surprised to find that that suggestion has been executed any morning; the violent preliminaries to such an event would not surprise me. I have done things lately that must be incomprehensible to the people, and which cannot now be explained."[9]

Congress too was growing disenchanted with the president. Michigan Senator Zachariah Chandler declared that "the country is gone for unless something is done at once." Lincoln, he concluded, "is a weak man, too weak for the occasion," and as "unstable as water."[10]

Rather than attack Lincoln directly, congressmen and senators, upset by the defeats at Fredericksburg and at the polls, made Seward their scapegoat. Anger at the secretary of state had been building for some time. In September, when a delegation from New York called at the White House to urge a change of policy, a "sharp encounter" developed between Lincoln and John E. Williams. Then James A. Hamilton criticized Seward's April 10, 1861, dispatch to Charles Francis Adams. The president, "in an excited manner," interrupted: "Sir! You are subjecting some letter of Mr. Seward's to an undue criticism in an undue manner."

Pointing to Williams and Hamilton, he added, "You gentlemen, to hang Mr. Seward, would destroy this government." Hamilton replied, "Sir, that is a very harsh remark."[11] Two months later, Congressman Thaddeus Stevens wrote that "it would be a great blessing if Seward could be removed."[12]

To achieve that end, thirty-two Republican senators, with the news of the Fredericksburg debacle fresh in their minds, caucused secretly on December 16 and 17 "to ascertain whether any steps could be taken to quiet the public mind and to produce a better condition of affairs." They denounced Seward bitterly "and charged him with all the disasters which had come upon our arms alleging that he was opposed to a vigorous prosecution of the war—controlled the President and thwarted the other members of the Cabinet." Lincoln, too, was criticized for failing "to consult his Cabinet councilors, as a body, upon important matters" and for appointing generals "who did not believe in the policy of the government and had no sympathy with its purposes."[13]

The senators' chief informant was Chase, the leader of the Radical faction in the cabinet; Seward represented the opposite end of the ideological spectrum. In their competition to win Lincoln's favor, Seward had proved victorious.[14] As Welles put it, "Seward's more pleasant nature and consummate skill have enabled him to get windward of Chase." The president, Welles confided to his diary, "is fond of Seward, who is affable. He respects Chase, who is clumsy. Seward comforts him. Chase he deems a necessity."[15]

The haughty Chase regarded both his cabinet colleagues and the president with lordly contempt and schemed to win the Republican presidential nomination in 1864. Lincoln told Frank P. Blair that the treasury secretary "runs the machine against me."[16] Chase called the secretary of state "a backstairs influence which often controlled the apparent conclusions of the cabinet itself" and told senators that there was "no cabinet except in name. The Heads of Departments come together now and then—nominally twice a week–; but no reports are made; no

regular discussions held; no ascertained conclusions reached. Sometimes weeks pass by and no full meeting is held."[17] A senator who was
convinced that the cabinet squabbled fiercely said, "Take seven cats, put
them together in a bag, sew up its mouth, and shake it up *well*—WELL,
mind you—and you have the Cabinet!"[18]

Fully aware of these comments and criticisms, Lincoln said "he had
no doubt that Chase was at the bottom of all the mischief, and was setting the radicals on to assail Seward."[19]

Nicolay and Hay describe Chase's character and the president's master-
ful defusing of the grave crisis precipitated by the treasury secretary
(*Abraham Lincoln: A History*, 6:253–73):

Mr. Seward and Mr. Chase became at an early day, and
continued to be, respectively, the representatives in the Cabinet
of the more conservative and the more radical elements of the
Republican party. Each exerted himself with equal zeal and
equal energy in the branch of the public service committed to
his charge; but their relative attitudes towards the President soon
became entirely different. Mr. Seward, while doing everything
possible to serve the national cause, and thus unconsciously
building for himself an enduring monument in the respect and
regard of the country, was, so far as can be discerned, absolutely
free from any ambition or afterthought personal to himself.
He was, during the early part of the war, so intent upon the
work immediately in hand that he had no leisure for political
combinations; and later, when the subject of the next Presidential nomination began to be considered and discussed, he
recognized the fact that Mr. Lincoln was best qualified by his
abilities, his experience, and his standing in the country to be
his own successor.

The attitude of Mr. Chase was altogether unlike this. . . . he
did all that man could do to grapple with the problem of supplying the ways and means of the gigantic war. With untiring
zeal and perfect integrity he devoted his extraordinary ability

to the work of raising the thousands of millions expended in the great struggle which was crowned with a colossal success. But his attitude towards the President, it is hardly too much to say, was one which varied between the limits of active hostility and benevolent contempt. He apparently never changed his opinion that a great mistake had been committed at [the 1860 Republican convention in] Chicago, and the predominant thought which was present to him through three years of his administration was that it was his duty to counteract, as far as possible, the evil results of that mistake.

He felt himself alone in the Cabinet. He looked upon the President and all his colleagues as his inferiors in capacity, in zeal, in devotion to liberty and the general welfare. He sincerely persuaded himself that every disaster which happened to the country happened because his advice was not followed, and that every piece of good fortune was due to his having been able, from time to time, to rescue the President and the rest of the Cabinet from the consequences of their own errors. He kept up a voluminous correspondence with friends in all sections of the country, to which we should hesitate to refer had it not been that he retained copies of his letters, and many years afterwards gave them into the hands of a biographer for publication. These letters are pervaded by a constant tone of slight and criticism towards his chief and his colleagues. He continually disavows all responsibility for the conduct of the war. In one letter he says: "Since the incoming of General Halleck I have known but little more of the progress of the war than any outsider—I mean so far as influencing it goes. My recommendations, before he came in, were generally disregarded, and since have been seldom ventured. . . . I hope for the best. Those who reject my counsels ought to know better than I do." To Senator [John] Sherman he wrote:

> The future does not look promising to me, though it may be brighter than it seems to be. Since General Halleck has been here the conduct of the war has been abandoned to him by the President almost absolutely. We, who are called members

of the Cabinet, but are in reality only separate heads of departments, meeting now and then for talk on whatever happens to come uppermost, not for grave consultation on matters concerning the salvation of the country—we have as little to do with it as if we were the heads of factories supplying shoes or clothing. No regular and systematic reports of what is done are made, I believe, even to the President; certainly none are made to the Cabinet. Of course we may hope the best; that privilege always remains. It is painful, however, to hear complaints of remissness, delays, discords, dangers, and feel that there must be ground for such complaints, and know, at the same time, that one has no power to remedy the evils complained of, and yet be thought to have.

To another he said: " . . . Though charged with the responsibility of providing means for the vast expenditures of the war, I have little more voice in its conduct than a stranger to the Administration; perhaps not so considerable a voice as some who are, in law, at least, strangers to it. I should be very well satisfied with this state of things if I saw the war prosecuted with vigor and success. I am only dissatisfied with it because I cannot help thinking that if my judgment had more weight it would be so prosecuted."

His letters in this strain are innumerable. In all of them he labors to keep himself distinct and separate from the rest of the Government, protesting against its faults and errors, and taking credit for the good advice he wastes upon them. He says:

We have fallen on very evil days. Under the influence of a short-sighted notion that the old Union can be reconstituted, after a year's civil war of free States and slave States, just as it was, the President has hitherto refused to sanction any adequate measure for the liberation of the loyal population of the South from slavery to the rebels. Hence we are fighting rebellion with one hand, and with the other supplying its vital elements of strength. Then we have placed and continued in command generals who have never manifested the slightest sympathy with our cause, as related to the controlling question of slavery. These naturally have never been more than half in earnest, and instead of their being impelled to the most vigorous action, their influence has been suffered to paralyze, in a great degree, the activity of the Administration. In addition to this there has been enormous waste and profusion growing out of high pay and excessive indulgence. All these causes tend to demoralization, and we are demoralized. I cannot go into particulars, but the instances abound. It is some consolation to me that my voice and, so far as opportunity has allowed, my example has been steadily opposed to all this. I have urged my ideas on the President and my associates, till I begin to feel that they are irksome to the first, and to one or two at least of the second.

All this time, with the most facile self-deception, he believed in his own loyalty and friendship for the President, and used to record in his diary his sorrow for Mr. Lincoln's fatal course. September 12 he writes:

> The Secretary [of War] informed me that he had heard from General Halleck that the President is going out to see General McClellan, and commented with some severity on his humiliating submissiveness to that officer. It is indeed humiliating, but prompted, I believe, by a sincere desire to serve the country. . . . I think that the President, with the most honest intentions in the world, and a naturally clear judgment and a true, unselfish patriotism, has yielded so much to border-State and negrophobic counsels that he now finds it difficult to arrest his own descent towards the most fatal concessions. He has already separated himself from the great body of the party which elected him; distrusts most those who represent its spirit, and waits—for what?

He says in another place: "September 11. How singularly all our worst defeats have followed administrative blunders. McDowell defeated at Bull Run, because the Administration would not supersede Patterson by a general of more capacity, vigor, and devotion to the cause; McClellan defeated at Richmond, because the Administration recalled [General James]

Shields and forced [General John C.] Fremont to retire from the pursuit of Jackson; . . . Pope defeated at Bull Run, because the Administration persisted in keeping McClellan in command of the Army of the Potomac."

He never lost an opportunity for ingratiating himself with the general in favor, or the general in disgrace. He paid equally assiduous homage to the rising and the setting sun. In the dawn of McClellan's first successes in the West he made haste to write to him: "The country was indebted to me . . . in some considerable degree for the change of your commission from Ohio into a commission of major-general of the army of the Union, and your assignment to the command of the Department of the Ohio. I drew with my own hand the order extending it into Virginia. . . . It was my wish that you should remain in command on the Mississippi, but in this I was overruled."

His present command, however, he says, is a more important one, and he wishes Kentucky and Tennessee to be included in it, and thinks both will be done. When McClellan was appointed general-in-chief the Secretary, eager to be first to tell the good news, immediately wrote a note to Colonel Key, McClellan's judge-advocate: "McClellan is Commander-in-Chief. Let us thank God and take courage." To newly appointed and promoted generals he wrote in the same strain. Even when he had become estranged from a prominent officer the slightest appeal to his *amour propre* was sufficient to bring about a reconciliation. After he had lost all confidence in McClellan, and almost given up the President for not dismissing him, General John Cochrane came to him and said McClellan would like to retire from active command if he could do so without disgrace—which could be accomplished, and a more active general secured, by restoring him to the chief command, "where he would now act in unison with myself," says the Secretary. He entered at once into *pourparlers*, saying how much he had once admired and confided in McClellan; how the general came to lose his confidence; how heartily he had supported him with supplies and reenforcements, notwithstanding his mistrust; his entire willingness to receive any correction which facts would warrant; his absolute freedom from personal ill-will. When Cochrane told him that Colonel [Thomas] Key had often expressed his regret that Mc-Clellan had not conferred and acted in concert with the Secretary, he replied: "I think if he had, that the rebellion would be ended now." Further letters followed between them which are recorded in his diary; but during these platonic negotiations McClellan was finally removed from command.

Mr. Chase cultivated, however, the closest relations with those generals who imagined they had a grievance against the Administration. He took General Shields to his arms when he returned from the Shenandoah after his disastrous experience with Jackson. Shields's account of how he would have destroyed Stonewall Jackson if the President had permitted him did not apparently touch the Secretary's sense of humor. He received it all in good faith; assured Shields that if he had had his way he should have been supported, and wrote in his diary: "Sad! sad! yet nobody seems to heed. General Shields and I talked all this over, deploring the strange fatality which seemed to preside over the whole transaction. He dined with us and after dinner rode out." To [General Joseph] Hooker, after the failure of the Chickahominy campaign, he said, "General, if my advice had been followed, you would have commanded [the army] after the retreat to James River, if not before"; to which Fighting Joe of course responded, "If I had commanded, Richmond would have been ours." He warmly sympathized with General [David] Hunter after the revocation of his emancipation order in South Carolina, and allowed his preference for military emancipation to carry him, in one instance, to the point of absolute disloyalty to the President. On the 31st of July, 1862, he wrote a long letter to General [Benjamin F.] Butler in New Orleans, striving to controvert the views of the President in relation to slavery in the Gulf States, and urging in place of them his own opinions, "to which," he said, "I am just as sure the masses will and the politicians must come, as I am sure that both politicians and masses have come, to opinions expressed by me when they found few concurrents"; and he continued his letter with this rash and mischievous advice: "Of course, if some prudential consideration did not forbid, I should at once, if I were in your place, notify the slaveholders of Louisiana that henceforth they must be content to pay their laborers wages. . . . It is quite true that such an order could not be enforced by military power beyond military lines, but it would enforce itself by degrees a good way beyond them, and would make the extension of military lines comparatively quite easy."

Here the obvious objection presented itself, that such a course would be in direct contravention to the President's known policy, and would be immediately repudiated and revoked by him. The Secretary foresaw this, and added a prediction so reckless, and so disloyal to his constitutional chief, that if it were not printed by undoubted authority it would be difficult to believe he had written it: "It may be said that such an order would be annulled. I think not. It is plain enough to see that the annulling of Hunter's order was a mistake. It will not be repeated." A volume could not more clearly show the Secretary's opinion of the President.

The surest way to his confidence and regard was to approach him with conversation derogatory to Mr. Lincoln. He records in his diary an after dinner conversation with an officer whom he seems to have met for the first time: "I then asked what he thought of the President." He apparently had no perception of the gross impropriety of such a question coming from him. The officer evidently knew what sort of reply was expected. He said: "A man irresolute, but of honest intentions; born a poor white, in a slave State, and of course among aristocrats; kind in spirit and not envious, but anxious for approval, especially of those to whom he has been accustomed to look up—hence solicitous of support of the slaveholders in the border States, and unwilling to offend them; without the large mind necessary to grasp great questions, uncertain of himself, and in many things ready to lean too much on others."

Of course, after a dictum so thoroughly in harmony with his own opinions, the Secretary naively records that he found this gentleman "well-read and extremely intelligent." In reply to a correspondent, whose letters were filled with the most violent abuse of the President and other officers of the Government, he had no word of rebuke. He simply replied: "I am not responsible for the management of the war and have no voice in it, except that I am not forbidden to make suggestions; and do so now and then when I can't help it."

He had no defense for his colleagues against the attacks of his correspondent, except to say: "Nor should you forget that a war managed by a President, a commanding general, and a Secretary cannot, especially when the great differences of temperament, wishes, and intellectual characteristics of these three are taken into account, reasonably be expected to be conducted in the best possible manner. This condition can only be remedied by the President, and, as yet, he fears the remedy most."

The President was not unaware of this disposition of his minister of finance towards him. Presidents in even a greater degree than kings are kept informed of all currents of favor and hostility about them; for besides being to an equal degree the source of honors and of power, they are not encompassed by any of that divinity which hedges the hereditary ruler, and they are compelled to listen to the crude truth from the hundreds of statesmen and politicians who surround them. And, besides this, the Secretary of the Treasury was a man too direct and too straightforward to work in the darkness. He records in his diary a singular conversation which he held with Thurlow Weed, an intimate and trusted counselor of the President and the bosom friend of the Secretary of State: "Weed called, and we had a long talk. . . . I told him I did not doubt Mr. Seward's fidelity to his ideas of progress, amelioration, and freedom, but that I thought he adhered too tenaciously to men who proved themselves unworthy and dangerous, such as McClellan; that he resisted too persistently decided measures; that his influence encouraged the irresolution and inaction of the President in respect to men and measures, although personally he was as decided as anybody in favor of vigorous prosecution of the war, and as active as anybody in concerting plans of action against the rebels."

There is no doubt that Mr. Weed would consider it his duty to communicate to his friends this disparaging view entertained of them by the Secretary of the Treasury; indeed, the context shows that this was expected; and when we consider that Mr. Chase talked and wrote in this strain to hundreds of people in regard to his associates, it is likely that they were as thoroughly aware of his opinions and utterances as if he had made them in Cabinet meeting. But Seward was, as the President once said of him, "a man without gall"; and it was the lifelong habit of Mr. Lincoln to disregard slights that were personal to himself. He had the greatest respect and admiration for Mr. Chase's capacity; he believed thoroughly in his devotion to the national cause, and seeing every day the proof of his pure and able management of the finances of the Government he steadily refused to consider the question of the Secretary's feelings towards himself.

It was near the end of the year 1862 that an incident occurred which threatened for a time to deprive the Government of the services of the Secretaries both of State and of the Treasury. A strong feeling of discontent, gradually ripening into one of hostility, had grown up in the Senate against Mr. Seward. It was founded principally upon the ground formulated by Mr. Chase in his interview with Weed, that he "adhered too tenaciously to men who proved themselves unworthy and dangerous, such as McClellan; that he resisted too persistently decided measures, and that his influence encouraged the irresolution and inaction of the President in respect to men and measures"; and Mr. Sumner, who had up to this time been rather friendly than otherwise to Mr. Seward, was suddenly brought into sympathy with his opponents by discovering in the diplomatic correspondence a phrase bracketing together the secessionists and the extreme antislavery men for equal condemnation and criticism.

The feeling against the Secretary of State at last attained such a height in the Senate that a caucus was called to consider the matter, which resulted in a vote being taken demanding of the President the dismissal of Mr. Seward from his Cabinet. As a matter of taste and expediency this resolution later in the evening was withdrawn and another adopted in its place requesting the President to reconstruct the Cabinet, in which, although

Mr. Seward's name was not mentioned, the intention of the Republican Senators remained equally clear. A committee was appointed to present the sense of the caucus to the President, but before this was carried into effect Senator Preston King of New York, meeting the Secretary of State, acquainted him with these proceedings, and he, with his son, the Assistant Secretary of State, at once offered their resignations to the President.

On the morning of the 19th of December, a committee of nine waited upon the President and presented him the resolutions adopted the day before. A long and earnest conference took place between the President and the Committee which was marked on both sides by unusual candor and moderation. They, one by one, attacked the Secretary of State, not for any specific wrongdoing, but for a supposed lukewarmness in the conduct of affairs, and especially for a lack of interest in the antislavery measures of the Administration, which they considered essential to a successful prosecution of the war. When the President reported this conference to his Cabinet afterwards he said, in his own peculiar imagery: "While they seemed to believe in my honesty, they also appeared to think that when I had in me any good purpose or intention Seward contrived to suck it out of me unperceived." The conference ended without other result than an appointment for the Committee to call again in the evening. Lincoln at once called the Cabinet together and laid the entire matter before them. He gave them distinctly to understand that in this proceeding he was not inviting or intimating that he desired the resignation of any of them; he said he could not afford to lose any of them; that he did not see how he could get on with a Cabinet composed of new material, and he dismissed the council with a request that they also should meet him that evening. The Committee and the Cabinet—Seward of course being absent—came together in accordance with the President's instructions, and each party was greatly surprised to find the other there. He was determined, however, to have a thorough and frank discussion, so that, hereafter, neither in his Government nor in the Senate should it be possible to say that there were any points between them concealed or unexplained. The President stated the case and read the resolutions of the Senators, commenting upon parts of it with some gentle severity.

A general discussion then took place, marked with singular frankness, both in the attack and the defense, [Jacob] Collamer and [William P.] Fessenden speaking with more mildness than the others, but [James] Grimes, [Charles] Sumner, and [Lyman] Trumbull attacking the cabinet generally, and Mr. Seward particularly, with considerable sharpness. The Cabinet defended themselves in general and their absent colleague with equal energy but with unruffled temper. Mr. Chase alone seemed to feel himself in a false position. As we have seen in his interview with Weed, he was in the habit of using precisely the same expressions in regard to the Secretary of State as those employed by the Senators. Brought to bay thus unexpectedly, and summoned to speak before both parties to the controversy, he naturally felt the embarrassment of the situation. He could not join the Senate in their attack upon the Administration and he could not effectively defend his colleagues in the presence of eight Senators, to all of whom he had probably spoken in derogation of the President and the Secretary of State. He protested with some heat against the attitude in which he was placed, and said he would not have come if he had expected to be arraigned.

When the fire of the discussion had burned itself out, Mr. Lincoln took a formal vote. "Do you, gentlemen," he said," still think Seward ought to be excused?" Grimes, Trumbull, Sumner, and [Kansas Senator Samuel C.] Pomeroy said "Yes." Collamer, Fessenden, and [Jacob] Howard declined to commit themselves. [Ira] Harris was opposed to it and [Benjamin F.] Wade was absent. The meeting broke up late at night, says Secretary Welles, "in a milder spirit than it met." The free talk had cleared the air somewhat, and both parties to the controversy respected each other more than before. As the Senators were retiring, Mr. Trumbull paused for a moment at the door, then, turning, walked rapidly back to the President and said to him privately, but with great vehemence, that the Secretary of the Treasury had held a very different tone the last time he had spoken with him.

The news of this stormy meeting quickly transpired, and the next morning there was great discussion and excitement in the town. The resignation of Seward was regarded as irrevocable, and all the amateur Cabinet-makers were busy in the preparation of a new Administration. The hopes of all the enemies of the Government were greatly stimulated by this indication of divided counsels, and the partisans of General McClellan in particular thought they saw in this conjuncture the occasion for his return to power. In fact, they felt so sure of his speedy restoration to command that they began to stipulate as the price of their adhesion to him that he should dictate his own terms on his return; that he must insist upon the disposal of all the important commands in the army. They imagined that the President would be so helpless that the friends of McClellan might demand any terms they thought good.

The President, though deeply distressed at the turn which affairs had taken, preserved his coolness and kept his own counsel. On the morning of the 20th, in the presence of several other members of the Cabinet who had called for further discussion of the crisis, the Secretary of the Treasury tendered his resignation.

He held the written paper in his hand, but did not advance to deliver it. The President stepped forward and took it with an alacrity that surprised and, it must be said, disappointed Mr. Chase. He then at once dismissed the meeting. He afterwards said, that from the moment when he saw Mr. Chase holding his resignation in his hand, his way was clear before him. He immediately sent an identical note to the Secretary of the Treasury and the Secretary of State, saying: "You have respectively tendered me your resignations as Secretary of State and Secretary of the Treasury of the United States. I am apprised of the circumstances which may render this course personally desirable to each of you; but after most anxious consideration my deliberate judgment is that the public interest does not admit of it. I therefore have to request that you will resume the duties of your Departments respectively."

The next morning Mr. Seward addressed a brief note to the President, dated at the Department of State, saying: "I have cheerfully resumed the functions of this Department, in obedience to your command"; and inclosed a copy of this note to the Secretary of the Treasury. Mr. Chase found his position not quite so simple as that of the Secretary of State. He did not follow Mr. Seward's example in returning to the Cabinet as promptly as he did in leaving it. He wrote him a brief letter, saying: "I have received your note, and also a call from Mr. Nicolay, to whom I have promised an answer to the President to-morrow morning. My reflections strengthen my conviction that being once more honorably out of the Cabinet no important public interest now requires my return to it. If I yield this judgment, it will be in deference to apprehensions which really seem to me unfounded. I will sleep on it."

He had seen in the face of the President the gratification which the tender of his resignation had imparted, and returning to his house, while not entirely comprehending what had happened, he seemed conscious that he had made a misstep. He wrote a letter to the President, from which we take a few paragraphs: "Will you allow me to say that something you said or looked when I handed you my resignation this morning made on my mind the impression that having received the resignations both of Governor Seward and myself you felt that you could relieve yourself from trouble by declining to accept either, and that this feeling was one of gratification."

He then went on to say that he was glad of any opportunity to promote the comfort of the President, but that he did not desire him to decline accepting his resignation. He said:

> Recent events have too rudely jostled the unity of your
> Cabinet and disclosed an opinion too deeply seated, and
> too generally received in Congress and in the country, to be
> safely disregarded, that the concord in judgment and action

essential to successful administration does not prevail among its members. By some the embarrassment of administration is attributed to me; by others, to Mr. Seward; by others still, to other heads of Departments. Now neither Mr. Seward nor myself is essential to you or to the country. We both earnestly wish to be relieved from the oppressive charge of our respective Departments, and we have both placed our resignations in your hands.

He concluded by saying he thought both himself and Mr. Seward could better serve the country at that time as private citizens than in the Cabinet. He did not immediately transmit this letter to the President, and after hearing from Mr. Seward that he had gone back to the Cabinet his suggestion that both would better retire was no longer practicable. After a Sunday passed in very serious consideration, he resolved to withdraw his resignation. He was unable, even then, to imitate the brevity of Mr. Seward's note. He sent to the President his note of the 20th inclosed in another, in which he said that reflection had not much, if at all, changed his original impression, but that it had led him to the conclusion that he ought in this matter to conform his action to the President's judgment. He would therefore resume his post as Secretary of the Treasury, ready, however, to retire at any moment if, in the President's judgment, the success of the Administration might be in the slightest degree promoted thereby.

The untrained diplomatist of Illinois had thus met and conjured away, with unsurpassed courage and skill, one of the severest crises that ever threatened the integrity of his Administration. He had to meet it absolutely unaided: from the nature of the case he could take no advice from those who were nearest him in the Government. By his bold and original expedient of confronting the Senators with the Cabinet, and having them discuss their mutual misunderstandings under his own eye, he cleared up many dangerous misconceptions, and, as usually happens when both parties are men of intelligence and goodwill, brought about a friendlier and more considerate feeling between his Government and the Republican leaders than had ever before existed. By placing Mr. Chase in such an attitude that his resignation became necessary to his own sense of dignity he made himself absolute master of the situation; by treating the resignations and the return to the Cabinet of both ministers as one and the same transaction he saved for the nation the invaluable services of both, and preserved his own position of entire impartiality between the two wings of the Union party.

The results of this achievement were not merely temporary. From that hour there was a certain loosening of the hitherto close alliance between Mr. Chase and the Republican opposition to the President, while a kind of comradeship, born of their joint sortie and reentrance into the Government, gave thereafter a greater semblance of cordiality to the relations between the Secretaries of State and of the Treasury. But above all, the incident left the President seated more firmly than ever in the saddle. When the Cabinet had retired, and the President remained with the resignation of Mr. Chase in his hands, he said to a friend who entered soon after, in one of those graphic metaphors so often suggested to him by the memories of his pioneer childhood, and which revealed his careless greatness perhaps more clearly than his most labored official utterances, "Now I can ride; I have got a pumpkin in each end of my bag."

Nearly a year later he said in a conversation relating to this matter: "I do not see how it could have been done better. I am sure it was right. If I had yielded to that storm and dismissed Seward the thing would all have slumped over one way, and we should have been left with a scanty handful of supporters. When Chase gave in his resignation I saw that the game was in my hands, and I put it through."

Though the opposition to Mr. Seward did not immediately come to an end, it never exhibited such vitality again, and its later manifestations were treated far more cavalierly by Mr. Lincoln.

He had even before this dismissed one very respectable committee from New York who had called to express an unfavorable opinion of the premier, by saying, with unwonted harshness, that they would be willing to see the country ruined if they could turn out Seward; and after this incident he never again allowed the Secretary of State to be attacked with impunity in his presence.

11

LINCOLN'S FAME

$\mathcal{L}$incoln's greatness was widely acknowledged even before his death, as the distinguished historian Hans Trefousse has recently shown.[1] After 1865, his fame grew dramatically, spreading around the globe. Leo Tolstoy's tribute, given during an interview in 1909, provides eloquent testimony to its universality. "Of all the great national heroes and statesmen of history Lincoln is the only real giant," Tolstoy told Count S. Stakelberg.

> Alexander, Frederick the Great, Caesar, Napoleon, Gladstone and even Washington stand in greatness of character, in depth of feeling and in a certain moral power far behind Lincoln. Lincoln was a man of whom a nation has a right to be proud; he was a Christ in miniature, a saint of humanity, whose name will live thousands of years in the legends of future generations. We are still too near to his greatness, and so can hardly appreciate his divine power; but after a few centuries more our posterity will find him considerably bigger than we do. His genius is still too strong and too powerful for the common understanding, just as the sun is too hot when its light beams directly on us.

One day the great Russian novelist met a tribal chief "living far away from civilized life in the mountains." The chief asked Tolstoy to tell his family and neighbors about famous historical figures. After regaling them with stories of Alexander, Caesar, Frederick the Great, and Napoleon,

Tolstoy stopped. "But you have not told us a syllable about the greatest general and greatest ruler of the world," the chief objected.

We want to know something about him. He was a hero. He spoke with a voice of thunder; he laughed like the sunrise, and his deeds were strong as the rock and as sweet as the fragrance of roses. The angels appeared to his mother and predicted that the son whom she would conceive would become the greatest the stars had ever seen. He was so great that he even forgave the crimes of his greatest enemies and shook brotherly hands with those who had plotted against his life. His name was Lincoln and the country in which he lived is called America, which is so far away that if a youth should journey to reach it he would be an old man when he arrived. Tell us of that man.

"I looked at them," Tolstoy recollected, "and saw their faces all aglow, while their eyes were burning. I saw that these rude barbarians were really interested in a man whose name and deeds had already become a legend. I told them of Lincoln and his wisdom, of his home life and youth. They asked me ten questions to one which I was able to answer. They wanted to know all about his habits, his influence upon the people and his physical strength." They "were very astonished to hear that Lincoln made a sorry figure on a horse and that he lived such a simple life."

Tolstoy thought that this

little incident proves how largely the name of Lincoln is worshipped throughout the world and how legendary his personality has become. Now, why was Lincoln so great that he overshadows all other national heroes? He really was not a great general like Napoleon or Washington; he was not such a skillful statesman as Gladstone or Frederick the Great; but his supremacy expresses itself altogether in his peculiar moral power and in the greatness of his character. He had come through many hardships and much experience to the realization that the greatest human achievement is love. He was what Beethoven was in music, Dante in poetry, Raphael in painting, and Christ in the philosophy of life. He aspired to be divine—and he was. It is natural that before he reached his goal he had to walk the highway of mistakes. But we find him, nevertheless, in every tendency true to one main motive, and that was to benefit mankind. He was one who wanted to be great through his smallness. If he had failed to become President he would be, no doubt, just as great as he is now, but only God would appreciate it. The judgment of the world is usually wrong in the beginning, and it takes centuries to correct it. But in the case of Lincoln the world was right from the start.

Tolstoy concluded that the "greatness of Napoleon, Caesar or Washington is only moonlight by the sun of Lincoln. His example is universal and will last thousands of years. Washington was a typical American, Napoleon was a typical Frenchman, but Lincoln was a humanitarian as broad as the world. He was bigger than his country—bigger than all the Presidents together." He "lived and died a hero, and as a great character he will live as long as the world lives. May his life long bless humanity!"[2]

Nicolay and Hay closed their work with an eloquent analysis of Lincoln's reputation (*Abraham Lincoln: A History*, 10:351–56):

It is not difficult to perceive the basis of this sudden and world-wide fame, nor rash to predict its indefinite duration. There are two classes of men whose names are more enduring than any monument—the great writers; and the men of great achievement, the founders of states, the conquerors. Lincoln has the singular fortune to belong to both these categories; upon these broad and stable foundations his renown is securely built. Nothing would have more amazed him while he lived than to hear himself called a man of letters; but this age has produced few greater writers. We are only recording here the judgment of his peers. Emerson ranks him with Aesop and Pilpay in his lighter moods, and says: "The weight and penetration of many passages in his letters, messages, and speeches, hidden now by the very closeness of their application to the moment, are destined to a wide fame. What pregnant definitions, what unerring common-sense, what foresight, and on great occasions what lofty, and more than national, what human tone! His brief speech at Gettysburg will not easily be surpassed by words on any recorded occasion."

His style extorted the high praise of French Academicians; [Charles Forbes, comte de] Montalembert commended it as a model for the imitation of princes. Many of his phrases form part of the common speech of mankind. It is true that in his writings the range of subjects is not great; he is concerned chiefly with the political problems of the time, and the moral considerations involved in them. But the range of treatment is remarkably wide; it runs from the wit, the gay humor, the florid eloquence of his stump speeches to the marvelous sententiousness and brevity of the letter to Greeley and the address at Gettysburg, and the sustained and lofty grandeur of the Second Inaugural.

The more his writings are studied in connection with the important transactions of his age the higher will his reputation stand in the opinion of the lettered class. But the men of study and research are never numerous; and it is principally as a man of action that the world at large will regard him. It is the story of his objective life that will forever touch and hold the heart of mankind. His birthright was privation and ignorance not peculiar to his family, but the universal environment of his place and time; he burst through those enchaining conditions by the force of native genius and will; vice had no temptation for him; his course was as naturally upward as the skylark's; he won, against all conceivable obstacles, a high place in an exacting profession and an honorable position in public and private life; he became the foremost representative of a party founded on an uprising of the national conscience against a secular wrong, and thus came to the awful responsibilities of power in a time of terror and gloom. He met them with incomparable strength and virtue. Caring for nothing but the public good, free from envy or jealous fears, he surrounded himself with the leading men of his party, his most formidable rivals in public esteem, and through four years of stupendous difficulties he was head and shoulders above them all in the vital qualities of wisdom, foresight, knowledge of men, and thorough comprehension of measures. Personally opposed, as the radicals claim, by more than half of his own party in Congress, and bitterly denounced and maligned by his open adversaries, he yet bore himself with such extraordinary discretion and skill, that he obtained for the Government all the legislation it required, and so impressed himself upon the national mind that without personal effort or solicitation he became the only possible candidate of his party for reelection, and was chosen by an almost unanimous vote of the Electoral Colleges.

His qualities would have rendered his administration illustrious even in time of peace; but when we consider that in addition to the ordinary work of the executive office he was forced to assume the duties of Commander-in-Chief of the National forces engaged in the most complex and difficult war of modern times, the greatness of spirit as well as the intellectual strength he evinced in that capacity is nothing short of prodigious. After times will wonder, not at the few and unimportant mistakes he may have committed, but at the intuitive knowledge of his business that he displayed. We would not presume to express a personal opinion in this matter. We use the testimony only of the most authoritative names. General W. T. Sherman has repeatedly expressed the admiration and surprise with which he has read Mr. Lincoln's correspondence with his generals, and his opinion of the remarkable correctness of his military views.

General W. F. Smith says: "I have long held to the opinion that at the close of the war Mr. Lincoln was the superior of his generals in his comprehension of the effect of strategic movements and the proper method of following up victories to their legitimate conclusions." General J. H. Wilson holds the same opinion; and Colonel Robert N. Scott, in whose lamented death the army lost one of its most vigorous and best-trained intellects, frequently called Mr. Lincoln "the ablest strategist of the war."

To these qualifications of high literary excellence, and easy practical mastery of affairs of transcendent importance, we must add, as an explanation of his immediate and world-wide fame, his possession of certain moral qualities rarely combined, in such high degree, in one individual. His heart was so tender that he would dismount from his horse in a forest to replace in their nest young birds which had fallen by the roadside; he could not sleep at night if he knew that a soldier-boy was under sentence of death; he could not, even at the bidding of duty or policy, refuse the prayer of age or helplessness in distress. Children instinctively loved him; they never found his rugged features ugly; his sympathies were quick and seemingly unlimited. He was absolutely without prejudice of class or condition. Frederick Douglass says he was the only man of distinction he ever met who never reminded him by word or manner of his color; he was as just and generous to the rich and well born as to the poor and humble—a thing rare among politicians. He was tolerant even of evil: though no man can ever have lived with a loftier scorn of meanness and selfishness, he yet recognized their existence and counted with them. He said one day, with a flash of cynical wisdom worthy of La Rochefoucauld, that honest statesmanship was the employment of individual meannesses for the public good. He never asked perfection of anyone; he did not even insist, for others, upon the high standards he set up for himself. At a time before the word was invented he was the first of opportunists. With the fire of a reformer and a martyr in his heart he yet proceeded by the ways of cautious and practical statecraft. He always worked with things as they were, while never relinquishing the desire and effort to make them better. To a hope which saw the Delectable Mountains of absolute justice and peace in the future, to a faith that God in his own time would give to all men the things convenient to them, he added a charity which embraced in its deep bosom all the good and the bad, all the virtues and the infirmities of men, and a patience like that of nature, which in its vast and fruitful activity knows neither haste nor rest.

A character like this is among the precious heirlooms of the Republic; and by a special good fortune every part of the country has an equal claim and pride in it. Lincoln's blood came from the veins of New England emigrants, of Middle State Quakers, of Virginia planters, of Kentucky pioneers; he himself was one of the men who grew up with the earliest growth of the Great West. Every jewel of his mind or his conduct sheds radiance on each portion of the nation. The marvelous symmetry and balance of his intellect and character may have owed something to this varied environment of his race, and they may fitly typify the variety and solidity of the Republic. It may not be unreasonable to hope that his name and his renown may be forever a bond of union to the country which he loved with an affection so impartial, and served, in life and in death, with such entire devotion.

Notes
Index

NOTES

PREFACE

1. John G. Nicolay and John Hay, *Abraham Lincoln: A History* (10 vols.; New York: Century, 1890), 1:xiii.

2. John Hay to William Dean Howells, Washington, 22 January 1890, in George Monteiro and Brenda Murphy, eds., *John Hay–Howells Letters: The Correspondence of John Milton Hay and William Dean Howells, 1861–1905* (Boston: Twayne, 1980), 96.

INTRODUCTION

1. Forty excerpts appeared in the *Century* between 1886 and 1890.

2. A. Mitchell to Richard Watson Gilder, New York, 28 March 1887, Century Collection, New York Public Library; *Life*, 17 March 1887. The following month, *Life* again poked fun at Nicolay and Hay:

> A new game which properly comes under the head of Sport is "Progressive Lincoln." A copy of the *Century Magazine* is placed on each of the play-tables, which are arranged as in Progressive Euchre. The players then proceed to find anything they can about Abraham Lincoln in the "History of the Martyred President" now running in the Magazine. Those who find five remarks about him first are declared winners and move forward, while those who fail retrogress, as in all the progressive games now so popular. The game is destined to become a great favorite with society people, but one precaution should always be taken. Chapters of the history which contain five allusions to the subject must be provided for the game, otherwise the evening is likely to go by without any winners, and drag correspondingly. (*Life*, 4 April 1887)

3. *Life*, 12 May 1887.

4. Harry E. Pratt, "Lincoln Literature," *Illinois Libraries* 24 (1942): 35.

5. Richard Watson Gilder, quoted in David C. Mearns, ed., *The Lincoln Papers: The Story of the Collection with Selections to July 4, 1861* (2 vols.; Garden City, N.Y.: Doubleday, 1948), 1:79.

6. William Roscoe Thayer, *The Life and Letters of John Hay* (2 vols.; Boston: Houghton Mifflin, 1915), 2:50.

7. Tyler Dennett, *John Hay: From Poetry to Politics* (New York: Dodd, Mead, 1934), 135–36.

8. Hay to Nicolay, New York, Friday (only day given—ca. 1889 or 1890), John Hay Papers, John Hay Library, Brown University (in a folder marked "Abraham Lincoln: A History, Correspondence with Gilder, Buel & Nicolay").

9. St. Gaudens, n.p., n.d., quoted in Helen Nicolay, *Lincoln's Secretary: A Biography of John G. Nicolay* (New York: Longmans, Green, 1949), 298.

10. Gilder to Nicolay, n.p., n.d., in Helen Nicolay, *Lincoln's Secretary*, 299.

11. Gilder to Nicolay and Hay, New York, 2 January 1890, John Hay Papers, John Hay Library, Brown University.

12. Hay to Nicolay, Cleveland, 10 August 1885, John Hay Papers, John Hay Library, Brown University.

13. John G. Nicolay and John Hay, *Abraham Lincoln: A History* (10 vols.; New York: Century, 1890), 6:24.

14. Nicolay and Hay, *Lincoln*, 6:193.

15. Stephen W. Sears, *George B. McClellan: The Young Napoleon* (New York: Ticknor and Fields, 1988), xii.

16. Nicolay and Hay, *Lincoln*, 1:x–xi, xiii.

17. Nicolay to Gilder, Washington, 24 January 1890, copy, Nicolay Papers, Library of Congress.

18. This was the first volume in a series titled *Campaigns of the Civil War* (New York: Scribner's, 1881).

19. Hay to Nicolay, Cleveland, 10 August 1885, John Hay Papers, John Hay Library, Brown University.

20. Nicolay and Hay, *Lincoln*, 3:31, 21.

21. Nicolay and Hay, *Lincoln*, 2:330.

22. Nicolay and Hay, *Lincoln*, 3:274.

23. Hay to Nicolay, Cleveland, 10 August 1885, John Hay Papers, John Hay Library, Brown University.

24. Nicolay and Hay, *Lincoln*, 1:133.

25. Nicolay and Hay, *Lincoln*, 1:88.

26. Herndon to Jesse W. Weik, Chicago, 2 January 1887, and Springfield, 22 January 1887, in Emanuel Hertz, ed., *The Hidden Lincoln: From the Letters and Papers of William H. Herndon* (New York: Viking, 1938), 152, 158.

27. Milton Hay to John Hay, Springfield, 8 February 1887, John Hay Papers, John Hay Library, Brown University.

28. Mearns, ed., *Lincoln Papers*, 1:74.

29. Hay to Robert Todd Lincoln, Cleveland, 27 January 1885, in Mearns, ed., *Lincoln Papers*, 1:75.

30. Hay to Gilder, 29 December [1886], Lincoln File, Huntington Library, San Marino, California.

31. See Michael Burlingame, *The Inner World of Abraham Lincoln* (Urbana: University of Illinois Press, 1994), 21, 42; John Y. Simon, *House Divided: Lincoln and His Father* (Fort Wayne: Louis A. Warren Lincoln Library and Museum, 1987).

32. Benjamin P. Thomas, *Portrait for Posterity: Lincoln and His Biographers* (New Brunswick, N.J.: Rutgers University Press, 1947), 112–15.

33. Hay, "The Early Life of Abraham Lincoln," 3, John Hay Papers, John Hay Library, Brown University.

34. Hay, "Early Life," 44.

35. Hay to Lincoln, 20 April 1885, in Mearns, ed., *Lincoln Papers*, 1:75.

36. Hay to Lincoln, 6 January 1886, in Mearns, ed., *Lincoln Papers*, 1:75.

37. Hay to William H. Herndon, Paris, 5 September 1866, in Michael Burlingame, ed., *At Lincoln's Side: John Hay's Civil War Correspondence and Selected Writings* (Carbondale: Southern Illinois University Press, 2000), 110.

38. Evelyn W. Symington Collection, Library of Congress; John Hay Papers, John Hay Library, Brown University. The "Abraham Lincoln and the Army of the Potomac" manuscript in the Library of Congress contains the following chapters: vol. 4, chap. 25; vol. 5, chaps. 9, 10, 20–24; vol. 6, chaps. 1, 7, 9, 10; vol. 7, chaps. 4, 8, 9; vol. 8, chap. 9. At Brown in a 317-page manuscript volume titled "Lincoln. The End of the Civil War" are drafts of vol. 7, chap. 16; vol. 8, chaps. 14, 15; vol. 9, chaps. 7, 10, 13, 14, 18; vol. 10, chaps. 2, 3, 8, 9, 12, 14–18. In addition, there are typescripts of vol. 6, chaps. 7, 9; vol. 8, chaps. 11, 12; vol. 10, chaps. 2, 4, 5. Hay also says in correspondence that he wrote chapter 8 of volume 9. Moreover, a 287-page draft of the first seventeen chapters of volume 1 is bound under the title "The Early Life of Abraham Lincoln." This seems to be a later draft than the scattered early chapters in the Lincoln Presidential Library at Springfield. Thus, Hay wrote at least 59 of the 224 chapters.

39. Mearns to Otto Eisenschiml, Washington, 2 October 1951, copy, Mearns Papers, Library of Congress.

40. Browning, interview by Nicolay, Springfield, 17 June 1875, in Michael Burlingame, ed., *An Oral History of Abraham Lincoln: John G. Nicolay's Interviews and Essays* (Carbondale: Southern Illinois University Press, 1996), 1.

41. Nicolay and Hay, *Lincoln*, 1:201.

42. Burlingame, ed., *Oral History of Lincoln*, 3.

43. See the passages in Browning's diary dated 29 and 31 July 1861, 3 March 1862, and 3 July 1875, which were made available to the public only in 1993, in Burlingame, ed., *At Lincoln's Side*, 185–87.

44. Burlingame, ed., *At Lincoln's Side*, 185–203.

45. Adam Badeau, "Was Mrs. Lincoln Insane?" New York *World*, 9 January 1887. A clipping of this article, which tells at great length the story of Mrs. Lincoln's irrational conduct in March 1865 at City Point, Virginia, is among Nicolay and Hay's notes for their biography (John Hay Papers, John Hay Library, Brown University).

46. Hay to Nicolay, Cleveland, 29 August 1885, John Hay Papers, John Hay Library, Brown University.

47. Gilder to Nicolay and Hay, New York, 16 June 1888, Nicolay Papers, Library of Congress; Nicolay to Hay, Washington, 22 June 1888, John Hay Papers, John Hay Library, Brown University. Nicolay's daughter Helen compiled such a volume, which appeared in 1912. Hay did write "Life in the White House in Lincoln's Time," which ran in the *Century* in November 1890, and a lecture that he gave in the 1870s titled "Washington in the Heroic Age," but he composed no other such sketches. These can be found in Burlingame, ed., *At Lincoln's Side*, 113–40.

48. *Harper's Monthly* 82 (February 1891): 478–82, reproduced in George Monteiro and Brenda Murphy, eds., *John Hay–Howells Letters: The Correspondence of John Milton Hay and William Dean Howells, 1861–1905* (Boston: Twayne, 1980), 141.

49. Lincoln to Hay, Chicago, 14 April 1888, Evelyn W. Symington Collection, Library of Congress.

50. Letter by Rhodes, Paris, n.d., quoted in Mearns, ed., *Lincoln Papers*, 1:80.

51. Nevins to Ida M. Tarbell, New York, 30 May 1939, Tarbell Papers, Allegheny College, Meadville, Pennsylvania.

52. Mearns, ed., *Lincoln Papers*, 1:81.

53. William E. Barton, "The Lincoln of the Biographers," *Transactions of Illinois State Historical Society*, vol. 36 (Springfield: Illinois State Historical Society, 1929), 103. Harry E. Pratt echoed Barton, calling the biography "an invaluable storehouse of authentic material" (Pratt, "Lincoln Literature," 35).

54. "Certainly they have the partisan attitude." J. C. Fitzpatrick to James G. Randall, Washington, 12 March 1935, Randall Papers, Library of Congress.

55. Pratt, "Lincoln Literature," 35.

56. Nicolay and Hay, *Lincoln*, 1:104–5.

57. Poole, quoted in Herndon to Jesse W. Weik, Chicago, 24 December 1886, in Hertz, ed., *Hidden Lincoln*, 151.

58. David Rankin Barbee to Stephen I. Gilchrist, Washington, 2 April 1933, quoted in William H. Townsend to Edward C. Stone, Lexington, Ky., 6 March 1945, copy, F. Lauriston Bullard Papers, Boston University.

59. Nicolay and Hay, *Lincoln*, 4:192.

60. Nicolay and Hay, *Lincoln*, 2:306–14.

61. Pratt, "Lincoln Literature," 35.

62. They declined a chance to buy the copies of the Herndon interviews that Ward Hill Lamon owned. Hay to Nicolay, New York, 18 September 1887,

John Hay Papers, John Hay Library, Brown University. They did make use of Lamon's biography, which was based mainly on those interviews.

63. Herndon to Weik, Springfield, 22 January 1887, in Hertz, ed., *Hidden Lincoln*, 157.

64. Stephenson, quoted in William Peterfield Trent et al., eds., *The Cambridge History of American Literature* (4 vols.; New York: G. P. Putnam's Sons, 1927), 3:378.

65. For these aspects of Lincoln, see Burlingame, *Inner World*, passim.

66. Herndon to Weik, Chicago, 2 January 1887, in Hertz, ed., *Hidden Lincoln*, 152.

67. Basler to Robert Gale, 5 and 15 February 1974, copies, Basler Papers, Library of Congress.

1. ELECTION DAY 1860 AND CABINET MAKING

1. Springfield correspondence by [Samuel R.] W[eed], 6 November, *Missouri Democrat* (St. Louis), 7 November 1860.

2. Springfield correspondence, 6 November, New York *Tribune*, 7 and 10 November 1860; Springfield correspondence by [Samuel R.] W[eed], 6 November, *Missouri Democrat* (St. Louis), 7 November 1860.

3. Springfield correspondence by A. C. C., 7 November, *Independent Democrat* (Concord, N.H.), 22 November 1860.

4. Springfield correspondence, 6 November, New York *Tribune*, 7 and 10 November 1860.

5. Springfield correspondence by Hay, 7 November, Providence (R.I.) *Journal*, 15 November 1860, in Michael Burlingame, ed., *Lincoln's Journalist: John Hay's Anonymous Writings for the Press, 1860–1864* (Carbondale: Southern Illinois University Press, 1998), 14; memorandum by Nicolay, 6 November 1860, in Michael Burlingame, ed., *With Lincoln in the White House: Letters, Memoranda, and Other Writings of John G. Nicolay, 1860–1865* (Carbondale: Southern Illinois University Press, 2000), 8; William H. Herndon to Jesse W. Weik, Springfield, 14 November 1885, Herndon-Weik Papers, Library of Congress; Springfield correspondence, 6 November, New York *Tribune*, 7 and 10 November 1860.

6. Springfield correspondence by [Samuel R.] W[eed], 6 November, *Missouri Democrat* (St. Louis), 7 November 1860.

7. Springfield correspondence by A. C. C., 7 November, *Independent Democrat* (Concord, N.H.), 22 November 1860.

8. Samuel R. Weed, "Hearing the Returns with Mr. Lincoln," New York *Times* Magazine, 14 February 1932 (written in the 1880s). See also Springfield correspondence by A. C. C., 7 November, *Independent Democrat* (Concord, N.H.), 22 November 1860.

9. Springfield correspondence by [Samuel R.] W[eed], 7 November, *Missouri Democrat* (St. Louis), 8 November 1860.

10. Springfield correspondence, 7 November, New York *Tribune*, 8 and 12 November 1860; Weed, "Hearing the Returns"; Springfield correspondence by [Samuel R.] W[eed], 7 November, *Missouri Democrat* (St. Louis), 8 November 1860.

11. Mrs. James C. Conkling to her son, Clinton Conkling, Springfield, 7 November 1860, in Harry E. Pratt, ed., *Concerning Mr. Lincoln, in which Abraham Lincoln Is Pictured as He Appeared to Letter Writers of His Time* (Springfield: Abraham Lincoln Association, 1944), 27–28.

12. Springfield correspondence by [Samuel R.] W[eed], 7 November, *Missouri Democrat* (St. Louis), 8 November 1860.

13. Weed, "Hearing the Returns."

14. George W. Brinkerhoff to Edward McPherson, Springfield, 19 November 1860, McPherson Papers, Library of Congress.

15. James A. Bayard to S. L. M. Barlow, Wilmington, Delaware, 4 October 1860, Barlow Papers, Huntington Library, San Marino, California; William Dusinberre, *Civil War Issues in Philadelphia, 1856–1865* (Philadelphia: University of Pennsylvania Press, 1965), 101.

16. Springfield correspondence, 7 November, New York *Tribune*, 8 and 12 November 1860; Henry Guest McPike in Walter B. Stevens, *A Reporter's Lincoln*, ed. Michael Burlingame (1916; Lincoln: University of Nebraska Press, 1998), 64–65.

17. Springfield correspondence, 7 November, New York *Tribune*, 8 and 12 November 1860; Weed, "Hearing the Returns with Mr. Lincoln"; Springfield correspondence by [Samuel R.] W[eed], 7 November, *Missouri Democrat* (St. Louis), 8 November 1860.

18. Springfield correspondence by [Samuel R.] W[eed], 7 November, *Missouri Democrat* (St. Louis), 8 November 1860.

19. Lincoln allegedly said this to the mayor of Springfield, Goyn A. Sutton. Statement by Frederic W. Sutton, the son of the mayor, Evanston, Illinois, 7 April 1926, copy enclosed in Oliver R. Barrett to Albert J. Beveridge, Chicago, 17 June 1926, Beveridge Papers, Library of Congress.

20. Sangamon County gave Lincoln 3556 (48.3 percent) and Douglas 3598 (48.9 percent). The Congressional race there saw the Republican candidate win 3628 (50 percent) and his opponent 3629 (50 percent). In the gubernatorial contest, Yates won 3609 (49.2 percent) and his opponent 3601 (49.1 percent). In the special House election in January 1859, the county gave the Republican candidate 1711 (44 percent) and his Democratic opponent 2817 (56 percent). In the 1856 presidential race, Frémont won 2232, Buchanan 2519. In the 1858 House race, the Republican won 2803 (47.3 percent) and the Democrat 3010 (50.8 percent). Howard W. Allen and Vincent A. Lacey, eds., *Illinois Elections, 1818–1990: Candidates and County Returns for President, Governor, Senate, and House of Representatives* (Carbondale: Southern Illinois University Press, 1992).

21. Springfield correspondence, 7 November, New York *Tribune*, 8 and 12 November 1860. Lincoln received 1395 votes to Douglas's 1326, Breckinridge's 31, and Bell's 16.

22. William H. Herndon's account in Caroline Dall, "Journal of a tour through Illinois, Wisconsin and Ohio, Oct. & Nov. 1866," entry for 29 October 1866, Dall Papers, Bryn Mawr College.

3. DISTRIBUTING PATRONAGE: 1861

1. Cleveland *Plain Dealer*, n.d., copied in the New York *Daily News*, 26 February 1861; Ari A. Hoogenboom, *Outlawing the Spoils: A History of the Civil Service Reform Movement, 1865–1883* (Urbana: University of Illinois Press, 1961), 1–7; Carl Russell Fish, *The Civil Service and the Patronage* (Cambridge: Harvard University Press, 1920), 173–85; Leonard D. White, *The Jacksonians: A Study in Administrative History, 1829–1861* (New York: Macmillan, 1954), 300–46.

2. "The Policy of the Administration," Cincinnati *Gazette*, 8 April 1861.

3. Cincinnati *Commercial*, n.d., copied in the *Illinois State Register* (Springfield), 25 March 1861.

4. *Frank Leslie's Illustrated Newspaper*, 20 April 1861.

5. Washington correspondence by "Occasional" [John W. Forney], 1 April, Philadelphia *Press*, 2 April 1861.

6. Harvey to Horace Greeley, Washington, 24 March [1861], Greeley Papers, New York Public Library.

7. Indianapolis *Journal*, n.d., copied in the Cincinnati *Commercial*, 24 August 1861.

8. Washington correspondence, 26 March, Charleston *Mercury*, 29 March 1861.

9. New York *Morning Express*, 1 April 1861.

10. One report said he arose at 6 A.M. and worked till well past midnight. Washington correspondence, 15 March, New York *Times*, 16 March 1861.

11. Washington correspondence by Sigma, 10, 11, and 12 March, Cincinnati *Commercial*, 11, 12, and 13 March 1861. His first excursion outside the White House occurred on March 12, when he took a brief walk around its grounds. Washington correspondence, 12 March, New York *World*, 13 March 1861. By March 23, he had only twice ridden out from the Executive Mansion. Washington correspondence, 23 March, New York *World*, 25 March 1861.

12. That day was March 13. Washington correspondence, 16 March, Philadelphia *Daily News*, 18 March 1861. On March 23 he declined receiving any callers.

13. Washington correspondence, 18 March, New York *Tribune*, 19 March 1861.

14. William Dean Howells, *Literary Friends and Acquaintances: A Personal Retrospect of American Authorship*, ed. David F. Hiatt and Edwin H. Cady

(1900; Bloomington: Indiana University Press, 1968), 73; William O. Stoddard, "Recollections of a Checkered Lifetime," unpublished memoirs, 2 vols.; 2:429, Detroit Public Library; Washington correspondence, 7 March, New York *Times*, 8 March 1861.

15. William O. Stoddard, "White House Sketches," New York *Citizen*, 25 August 1866, in Stoddard, *Inside the White House in War Times: Memoirs and Reports of Lincoln's Secretary*, ed. Michael Burlingame (1890; Lincoln: University of Nebraska Press, 2000), 151, 57; Robert Colby to Lincoln, New York, 18 May 1861, Lincoln Papers, Library of Congress; Washington correspondence by Noah Brooks, 7 November, Sacramento *Daily Union*, 4 December 1863, in Michael Burlingame, ed., *Lincoln Observed: Civil War Dispatches of Noah Brooks* (Baltimore: Johns Hopkins University Press, 1998), 83.

16. John Russell Young, "Lincoln as He Was," Pittsburgh *Dispatch*, 23 August 1891.

17. Stoddard, "White House Sketches," New York *Citizen*, 25 August 1866, in Stoddard, *Inside the White House*, ed. Burlingame, 151, 57.

18. John W. Starr, "Lincoln and the Office Seekers," typescript dated 1936, addenda, p. 6, Lincoln files, "Patronage" folder, Lincoln Memorial University, Harrogate, Tennessee. A Washington paper reported that Lincoln "is almost daily annoyed by victims of insanity, who deem their opinions and advice to be of vast importance to the interests of the nation." Washington *Sunday Chronicle*, 24 November 1861. Sometimes they were arrested for disorderly conduct. Washington correspondence, 3 December, New York *Herald*, 4 December 1862.

19. John Russell Young, "John Hay, Secretary of State," *Munsey's Magazine*, 8 January 1929, 247; Young in the Philadelphia *Evening Star*, 22 August 1891; Young, writing in 1898, quoted in T. C. Evans, "Personal Reminiscences of John Hay," Chattanooga (Tenn.) *Sunday Times*, 30 July 1905. Commenting on the August 1891 article, Hay told Young, "I read what you say of me, with the tender interest with which we hear a dead friend praised. The boy you describe in such charming language was once very dear to me—and although I cannot rate him so highly as you do, I am pleased and flattered more than I can tell you to know he made any such impression on a mind like yours." Hay to Young, Newbury, New Hampshire, 27 August 1891, Young Papers, Library of Congress. On the relationship between Hamilton and Washington, see Ron Chernow, *Alexander Hamilton* (New York: Penguin, 2004).

20. J. B. Angell, *The Reminiscences of James Burrill Angell* (New York: Longmans, Green, 1912), 109.

21. A. S. Chapman, "The Boyhood of John Hay," *Century Magazine*, July 1909, 450.

22. William Leete Stone, "John Hay, 1858," in *Memories of Brown: Traditions and Recollections Gathered from Many Sources*, ed. Robert Perkins Brown et al. (Providence, R.I.: Brown Alumni Magazine, 1909), 153–54.

23. Bishop, "A Friendship with John Hay," *Century Magazine*, March 1906, 778.

24. Clark E. Carr, *The Illini: A Story of the Prairies* (Chicago: McClurg, 1904), 51.

25. Logan Hay's "Notes on the History of the Logan and Hay Families," 30 May 1939, Stuart-Hay Papers, Lincoln Presidential Library.

26. St. Louis *Dispatch*, 30 May [no year given], clipping in a scrapbook, John Hay Papers, John Hay Library, Brown University.

27. Mitchel to Hay, East Orange, New Jersey, 12 February 1905, John Hay Papers, John Hay Library, Brown University.

28. David Herbert Donald, *"We Are Lincoln Men": Abraham Lincoln and His Friends* (New York: Simon and Schuster, 2003), 177–211.

29. "The Authorship of the Bixby Letter," in Michael Burlingame, ed., *At Lincoln's Side: John Hay's Civil War Correspondence and Selected Writings* (Carbondale: Southern Illinois University Press, 2000), 169–84.

30. John Hay to James A. Garfield, Washington, 16 February 1881, John Hay Papers, John Hay Library, Brown University.

31. Washington correspondence by John Hay, 6 March, New York *World*, 8 March 1861, in Burlingame, ed., *Lincoln's Journalist*, 54.

32. "A Disappointed Office-seeker Discourseth to his Brothers," Washington, 20 March, New York *Evening Post*, 26 March 1861.

33. Schuyler Colfax to [Daniel D. Pratt], Washington, 7 December 1860, Pratt Papers, Indiana State Library, Indianapolis.

34. Washington correspondence, 1 April, Cincinnati *Commercial*, 3 April 1861; Washington correspondence, 31 March, New York *World*, 1 April 1861; Nicolay to Therena Bates, Washington, 31 March and 2 April 1861, in Burlingame, ed., *With Lincoln in the White House*, 32.

35. Hay to William H. Herndon, Paris, 5 September 1866, in Burlingame, ed., *At Lincoln's Side*, 109; Washington correspondence, 17 March, New York *Times*, 18 March 1861.

36. Washington correspondence, 12, 22 March, Cincinnati *Gazette*, 13, 25 March 1861.

37. Washington correspondence by Sigma, 10 March, Cincinnati *Commercial*, 11 March 1861.

38. Washington correspondence by Kritick, 14 March, Charleston *Courier*, 18 March 1861; Washington correspondence, 18 March, New York *Herald*, 19 March 1861; Washington correspondence, 17 March, New York *Evening Post*, 18 March 1861.

39. "A Disappointed Office-seeker Discourseth to his Brothers," Washington, 20 March, New York *Evening Post*, 26 March 1861.

40. Washington correspondence, 15 March, New York *Evening Post*, 16 March 1861. Cf. Washington correspondence, 13 March, New York *Tribune*, 14 March 1861.

41. Washington correspondence by Sigma, 14 March, Cincinnati *Commercial*, 15 March 1861.

42. Washington correspondence, 24 March, Philadelphia *Press*, 25 March 1861.

43. Stanton to James Buchanan, Washington, 3 April 1861, Buchanan Papers, Historical Society of Pennsylvania.

44. Washington correspondence, 3 April, Cincinnati *Enquirer*, n.d., copied in the *Illinois State Register* (Springfield), 5 April 1861.

45. "Physical Theory of the Presidency," New York *Times*, 4 April 1861.

46. Francis B. Carpenter, *Six Months at the White House with Abraham Lincoln* (New York: Hurd and Houghton, 1867), 276.

47. Schurz to his wife, Alton, 25 July 1860, in Frederic Bancroft, ed., *Speeches, Correspondence and Political Papers of Carl Schurz* (6 vols.; New York: G. P. Putnam's Sons, 1913), 1:120.

48. Robert Wilson to William H. Herndon, Sterling, Illinois, 10 February 1866, in Douglas L. Wilson and Rodney O. Davis, eds., *Herndon's Informants: Letters, Interviews, and Statements about Abraham Lincoln* (Urbana: University of Illinois Press, 1998), 206–7.

49. Washington correspondence, 31 March, New York *Evening Post*, 1 April 1861.

50. Adam Gurowski, *Diary* (3 vols.; Boston, 1862–66) 1:16–17 (section headed March 1861). Attorney General Edward Bates gave posts to his Missouri friends. Marvin R. Cain, *Lincoln's Attorney General: Edward Bates of Missouri* (Columbia: University of Missouri Press, 1965), 130. Treasury Secretary Salmon P. Chase gave posts to his Ohio friends. John Niven, *Salmon P. Chase: A Biography* (New York: Oxford University Press, 1995), 239–42. Secretary of War Simon Cameron gave posts to his Pennsylvania friends. Erwin Stanley Bradley, *Simon Cameron, Lincoln's Secretary of War: A Political Biography* (Philadelphia: University of Pennsylvania Press, 1966), 179–81.

51. Sarah A. Wallace and Frances E. Gillespie, eds., *The Journal of Benjamin Moran, 1857—1865* (2 vols.; Chicago: University of Chicago Press, 1949), 2:1092 (entry for 19 November 1862); Charles Francis Adams diary, 1 May 1865, Adams Family Papers, Massachusetts Historical Society.

52. Horace White, "Introduction," William H. Herndon and Jesse W. Weik, *Abraham Lincoln: The True Story of a Great Life* (2 vols.; New York: Appleton, 1909), 1:xxi–xxii.

53. Wallace and Gillespie, eds., *Moran Journal,* 2:909 (20 November 1861).

54. Welles, quoted in Harry J. Carman and Reinhard H. Luthin, *Lincoln and the Patronage* (New York: Columbia University Press, 1943), 336.

55. Carl Russell Fish, "Lincoln and the Patronage," *American Historical Review* 8 (1902): 54, 68; Fish, *Civil Service*, 168–72; Carman and Luthin, *Lincoln and the Patronage*, 335–36.

4. FRONTIER GUARDS AT THE WHITE HOUSE: APRIL 1861

1. Allan Nevins, *The War for the Union* (4 vols.; New York: Scribner's, 1959–71), 1:79.

2. Edward A. Miller, *Lincoln's Abolitionist General: The Biography of David Hunter* (Columbia: University of South Carolina Press, 1997), 54–57.

3. David L. Smiley, *Lion of White Hall: The Life of Cassius M. Clay* (Madison: University of Wisconsin Press, 1962), 175–76.

4. Michael Burlingame and John R. Turner Ettlinger, eds., *Inside Lincoln's White House: The Complete Civil War Diary of John Hay* (Carbondale: Southern Illinois University Press, 1997), 8 (entry for 22 April 1861).

5. Miller, *Lincoln's Abolitionist General*, 55–57.

6. *Kansas State Journal* (Lawrence), 9 May 1861.

7. Washington *Evening Star*, 19 April 1861.

8. Ward Hill Lamon's reminiscences, Washington *Evening Star*, 24 May 1890.

9. Constance M. Green, *Washington* (2 vols.; Princeton: Princeton University Press, 1962–63), 1:241.

10. Nicolay to Therena Bates, Washington, 19 April 1861, in Michael Burlingame, ed., *With Lincoln in the White House: Letters, Memoranda, and Other Writings of John G. Nicolay, 1860–1865* (Carbondale: Southern Illinois University Press, 2000), 35.

11. Washington correspondence, 17 April, New York *Times*, 18 April 1861.

12. Washington *Evening Star*, 19 April 1861; Benjamin Franklin Cooling, *Symbol, Sword, and Shield: Defending Washington during the Civil War* (2nd rev. ed.; Shippensburg, Pa.: White Mane, 1991), 22–24.

13. Willis R. Copeland, *The Logan Guards of Lewistown, Pennsylvania: Our First Defenders of 1861* (Lewistown: Mifflin County Historical Society, 1962), 23; Oliver Christian Bosbyshell, "When and Where I Saw Lincoln," in John P. Nicholson, ed., *Abraham Lincoln* (Military Order of the Loyal Legion of the United States, Commandery of the State of Pennsylvania, Memorial Meeting, 13 February 1907), 17–18.

14. Bosbyshell, "When and Where I Saw Lincoln," 17–18; Heber S. Thompson, *The First Defenders* (n.p., 1910), 151.

5. WASHINGTON BESIEGED: APRIL 1861

1. The first troops wounded in the war were Pennsylvania militiamen attacked on April 18 by a mob in Baltimore.

2. Charles Branch Clark, "Baltimore and the Attack on the Sixth Massachusetts Regiment, 19 April 1861," *Maryland Historical Magazine* 56 (1961): 39–71; Frank Towers, "'A Vociferous Army of Howling Wolves': Baltimore's Civil War Riot of 19 April 1861," *Maryland Historical Magazine* 23 (1992): 1–27.

3. New York *Times*, 25 April 1861; Scott S. Sheads, *Baltimore during the Civil War* (Linthicum, Md.: Toomey Press, 1997), 153–54.

4. Thomas B. Lowry of Philadelphia described the president's reaction. Philadelphia *Press*, 22 April, copied in the New York *Times*, 23 April 1861. Lowry was the first to tell Lincoln of the attack on the Massachusetts troops.

5. Telegrams from George W. Brown and Thomas H. Hicks to Lincoln, 18, 19 April 1861, Lincoln Papers, Library of Congress. It is easy to see how Lincoln might have misinterpreted this language in the telegram of the 18th: "A collision between the citizens & the Northern troops has taken place in Baltimore and the excitement is fearful. Send no more troops here. We will endeavor to prevent all bloodshed A public meeting of citizens has been called and the troops of the State in the City have been called out to preserve the peace. They will be enough."

6. Michael Burlingame and John R. Turner Ettlinger, eds., *Inside Lincoln's White House: The Complete Civil War Diary of John Hay* (Carbondale: Southern Illinois University Press, 1997), 3 (entry for 19 April 1861).

7. Edward F. Jones to Daniel Butterfield, Binghamton, New York, 19 April 1901, in Julia Lorrilard Butterfield, *A Biographical Memorial of General Daniel Butterfield* (New York: Grafton Press, 1904), 29.

8. William Schouler, *A History of Massachusetts in the Civil War* (2 vols.; Boston: E. P. Dutton, 1868–71), 1:103–5.

9. Roy P. Basler et al., eds., *The Collected Works of Abraham Lincoln* (8 vols. plus index; New Brunswick, N.J.: Rutgers University Press, 1953–55), 4:340; Nicolay, memorandum of events, 19 April 1861, in Michael Burlingame, ed., *With Lincoln in the White House: Letters, Memoranda, and Other Writings of John G. Nicolay, 1860–1865* (Carbondale: Southern Illinois University Press, 2000), 34–35; Burlingame and Ettlinger, *Inside Lincoln's White House*, 5 (entry for 21 April 1861).

10. Nicolay, memoranda of events, 20, 21 April 1861, in Burlingame, ed., *With Lincoln in the White House*, 36, 37.

11. Baltimore *Exchange*, n.d., copied in the Cincinnati *Commercial*, 30 April 1861.

12. Nicolay, memorandum of events, 21 April 1861, in Burlingame, ed., *With Lincoln in the White House*, 38.

13. Washington correspondence by [George W.] S[imonton], 1 May, New York *Times*, 4 May 1861; George W. Brown, *Baltimore and the Nineteenth of April 1861: A Study of the War* (Baltimore: N. Murray, 1887), 71–74; George M. Brown's statement, dated Baltimore, 7:30 P.M., 21 April, Washington *National Intelligencer*, 22 April 1861; Nicolay, memorandum of events, 21 April 1861, in Burlingame, ed., *With Lincoln in the White House*, 37. Brown's version of Lincoln's remarks was deemed inaccurate by a correspondent for the New York *Times*, who reported that the Baltimoreans "strangely misunderstood or grossly perverted his language." Washington correspondence, 28 April, New York *Times*, 1 May 1861.

14. Mark Howard to Gideon Welles, Hartford, 25 April 1861, Welles Papers, Library of Congress; E. Seeley to Welles, New York, 25 April 1861, Welles Papers; Washington correspondence by Ben: Perley Poore, 26 April, Boston *Evening Journal*, 2 May 1861; Philadelphia correspondence, 23 April, New York *Tribune*, 24 April 1861.

15. William Faxon to Mark Howard, Washington, 12 May [1862], Mark Howard Papers, Connecticut Historical Society, Hartford.

16. Burlingame and Ettlinger, eds., *Inside Lincoln's White House*, 8 (entry for 23 April 1861).

17. Andrew H. Reeder to Simon Cameron, Philadelphia, 24 April 1861, Lincoln Papers, Library of Congress.

18. W. B. Smith to Chase, [Geneva,] 20 May 1861, Chase Papers, Library of Congress.

19. "The Administration's View of the War," New York *Tribune*, 25 April 1861; "A Startling Report," "Clear the Track!" and "The Government and the People," New York *Times*, 24, 26, 27 April 1861; "To Be Impeached," New York *Daily News*, 25 April 1861; "The New York *Times* and the Administration," New York *World*, 10 May 1861.

20. Washington correspondence, 1 May, New York *Tribune*, 2 May 1861.

21. Lincoln's endorsement on New York *Times* articles, 25 April 1861, Lincoln Papers, Library of Congress.

22. Washington correspondence by "Van" [D. W. Bartlett], 18 September, Springfield, Massachusetts, *Republican*, 21 September 1861.

23. New York *Times*, 25 April 1861.

24. Fuller to Chase, Baltimore, 23 April 1861, Chase Papers, Library of Congress. Fuller owned a large plantation in South Carolina.

25. Burlingame and Ettlinger, eds., *Inside Lincoln's White House*, 5, 6 (entries for 21, 22 April 1861).

26. This is a conflation of the following sources: Basler, ed., *Collected Works of Lincoln*, 4:341–42, which reproduces what Nicolay and Hay give in their biography of Lincoln; an account in the Baltimore *Sun*, 23 April 1861, evidently based on what Fuller told someone; Washington correspondence, 24 April, New York *Times*, 27 April 1861; and William Cullen Bryant's dispatch dated New York, 24 April, New York *Evening Post*, 24 April 1861. "Haggle" in this case means to cut clumsily or to hack.

27. Washington correspondence, n.d., Philadelphia *Gazette*, n.d., copied in the Chicago *Tribune*, 28 September 1861. This took place on a Saturday, presumably in late September.

28. John Pendleton Kennedy journal, 21 April 1861, Kennedy Papers, Enoch Pratt Free Library, Baltimore.

29. Washington correspondence by G. W. A., 29 April, Cincinnati *Gazette*, 3 May 1861. Similar sentiments were expressed by many of Salmon P. Chase's correspondents. See, for example, Erastus Hopkins to Chase, Northampton,

Massachusetts, 25 April 1861; Milton Sutliff to Chase, Cincinnati, 28 April 1861; S. Lester Taylor to Chase, Covington, Kentucky, 30 April 1861; Roswell Marsh to Chase, Steubenville, 4 May 1861, Chase Papers, Library of Congress.

30. Granville Moody to Chase, Cincinnati, 30 April 1861, Chase Papers, Library of Congress.

31. Andrew H. Reeder to Simon Cameron, Philadelphia, 24 April 1861, Lincoln Papers, Library of Congress.

32. Washington correspondence, 22 April, New York *Tribune*, 26 April 1861.

33. New York correspondence by A[lbert] D. R[ichardson], 24 April, New York *Tribune*, 25 April 1861.

34. New York *Tribune*, 2 May 1861.

35. Chase to Lincoln, Washington, 25 April 1861, Lincoln Papers, Library of Congress.

36. Reverdy Johnson to Lincoln, Washington, 23 April 1861, Lincoln Papers, Library of Congress; Basler, ed., *Collected Works of Lincoln*, 4:342–43. Johnson continued to warn against stationing troops in Baltimore. Reverdy Johnson to Chase, n.p., 8 May 1861, Chase Papers, Library of Congress.

37. Basler, ed., *Collected Works of Lincoln*, 5:24.

38. Nevins, *War for the Union*, 1:107–11; A. Howard Meneely, *The War Department, 1861: A Study in Mobilization and Administration* (New York: Columbia University Press, 1928), 106.

39. Magruder's reminiscences, taken from an unpublished memoir, edited by his brother, Allan B. Magruder, Philadelphia *Weekly Times*, 28 December 1878; Samuel D. Sturgis to the editor of the Philadelphia *Evening Telegraph*, 12 June 1870, draft, Sturgis Papers, in Don E. Fehrenbacher and Virginia Fehrenbacher, eds., *Recollected Words of Abraham Lincoln* (Stanford: Stanford University Press, 1996), 431–32; Burlingame and Ettlinger, eds., *Inside Lincoln's White House*, 5 (entry for 21 April 1861); Magruder to an unidentified resident of Philadelphia, Galveston, 8 May 1870, Philadelphia *Evening Telegraph*, n.d., copied in the New York *Times*, 23 May 1870. In his 1870 letter, Magruder remembered events quite differently, claiming that he had told the president he intended to join the Confederacy and that Lincoln had expressed his understanding.

40. Francis P. Blair Sr. to William Cullen Bryant, 5 August 1866, draft, Blair Family Papers, Library of Congress.

41. Lincoln, 4 July 1861 message to Congress, first draft, Lincoln Papers, Library of Congress. Actually, twenty-six enlisted men resigned to join the Confederacy. Meneely, *War Department*, 106.

42. Burlingame and Ettlinger, eds., *Inside Lincoln's White House*, 11 (entry for 24 April 1861).

43. Nicolay to Therena Bates, Washington, 26 April 1861, in Burlingame, ed., *With Lincoln in the White House*, 39–40.

44. Philadelphia correspondence, 23 April, New York *Tribune*, 24 April 1861; Washington correspondence by "Occasional" (John W. Forney), 21 April, Philadelphia *Press*, 24 April 1861; Washington correspondence by Ben: Perley Poore, 21 April, Boston *Journal*, 25 April 1861.

45. Burlingame and Ettlinger, eds., *Inside Lincoln's White House*, 8 (entry for 22 April 1861); Washington correspondence, 22 April, Baltimore *Sun*, 23 April 1861.

46. Washington correspondence, 28 April, New York *Times*, 1 May 1861; reminiscences of E. A. Spring, unidentified clipping with date 1898 penciled in, Lincoln Museum, Fort Wayne, Indiana; Washington correspondence, 25 April, New York *Tribune*, 26 April 1861; Washington correspondence, 25 April, New York *World*, 30 April 1861; Washington correspondence, 1 May, Cincinnati *Commercial*, 2 May 1861; Washington correspondence, 15 May, Springfield, Massachusetts, *Republican*, 17 May 1861.

6. THE FIRST BATTLE OF BULL RUN: JULY 21, 1861

1. Washington correspondence by Special, 31 May, Cincinnati *Commercial*, 1 June 1861.

2. Don E. Fehrenbacher, "Lincoln's Wartime Leadership: The First Hundred Days," *Journal of the Abraham Lincoln Association* 9 (1987): 15.

3. David W. Miller, *Second Only to Grant: Quartermaster General Montgomery C. Meigs: A Biography* (Shippensburg, Pa.: White Mane Books, 2000), 102.

4. McDowell's testimony, Committee on Conduct of the War, *Reports* (8 vols.; Washington, 1863–66), 2:38.

5. Meigs diary, 25 June 1861, copy, Nicolay Papers, Library of Congress.

6. McDowell's testimony, Committee on Conduct of the War, *Reports*, 2:36–38.

7. Meigs diary, 29 June 1861.

8. Reminiscences of Schuyler Hamilton, quoted in J. H. Stine, *A History of the Army of the Potomac* (Philadelphia: J. B. Rodgers, 1892), 7–10; E. D. Townsend, *Anecdotes of the Civil War in the United States* (New York: D. Appleton, 1884), 57; Charles Winslow Elliott, *Winfield Scott: The Soldier and the Man* (New York: Macmillan, 1937), 727–28; McDowell's testimony, Committee on Conduct of the War, *Reports* 2:35–38; Gen. Charles W. Sanford's testimony, Committee on Conduct of the War, *Reports*, 2:55, 62.

9. Colin R. Ballard, *The Military Genius of Abraham Lincoln: An Essay* (London: Oxford University Press, 1926), 56–59.

10. Reminiscences of Gary W. Hazleton, Edward S. Bragg Papers, Palmer Collection, Western Reserve Historical Society, copy, Allan Nevins Papers, Columbia University.

11. Russell H. Beatie, *Army of the Potomac: Birth of Command, November 1860–September 1861* (New York: Da Capo, 2002), 326. Scott and Lincoln

conferred at length on the morning of July 20. Washington correspondence, 20 July, New York *Tribune*, 21 July 1861.

12. Nicolay to Therena Bates, Washington, 21 July 1861, in Burlingame, ed., *With Lincoln in the White House*, 51.

7. LINCOLN AND SECRETARY OF WAR EDWIN M. STANTON

1. R. W. Bush to Joseph Holt, Louisville, 13 November 1861, Holt Papers, Library of Congress; Joshua Speed to Holt, Washington, 8 December 1861, Holt Papers.

2. Cameron interviewed by Nicolay, Washington, 20 February 1875, in Michael Burlingame, ed., *An Oral History of Abraham Lincoln: John G. Nicolay's Interviews and Essays* (Carbondale: Southern Illinois University Press, 1996), 44. See also Nevins, *War for the Union*, 1:408–9.

3. *McCormick v. Talcott et al.* (1854–55), in Martha L. Benner, Cullom Davis et al., eds., *The Law Practice of Abraham Lincoln* (DVD, University of Illinois Press, 2000), case file no. 02341; Harry Goldsmith, "Abraham Lincoln, Inventions and Patents," *Journal of the Patent Office Society* 20 (January 1938): 5–33; Emerson Hinchliff, "Lincoln and the 'Reaper Case,'" *Journal of the Illinois State Historical Society* 33 (September 1940): 361–65; "The Manny Reaper: Some Background Information on the Case of McCormick v. Manny, 1855," *Lincoln Lore* (June 1964): 1–4; Robert Henry Parkinson, "The Patent Case That Lifted Lincoln into a Presidential Candidate," *Abraham Lincoln Quarterly* 4 (September 1946): 105–22.

4. Letter by Mary Manny Tinker, Rockford, Illinois, 21 [*sic*] July 1896, *Rockford Register-Gazette*, 20 July 1896. In an obituary of Wait Talcott, at that time business manager of the Manny Company, it was reported that Lincoln's retainer was $1000. *Farm Implement News* (Chicago), December 1890, reprinted in the issue of 23 July 1896, 18.

5. Harding told this to Parkinson in 1876. Parkinson, "Patent Case," 113–15. See also George Alfred Townsend, "They Snubbed Lincoln," Cincinnati *Enquirer*, n.d. [1884], copied in an unidentified newspaper, clipping collection, Lincoln Museum, Fort Wayne, Indiana; and Harding's recollections given in a talk in the spring of 1895 at a smoker of the Sharswood Law Club, typescript, Henry B. Rankin Papers, vol. 9, Lincoln Presidential Library, Springfield.

6. Harding's recollections in Parkinson, "Patent Case," 115–16.

7. William M. Dickson to Jesse W. Weik, Cincinnati, 17 April 1888, in Douglas L. Wilson and Rodney O. Davis, eds., *Herndon's Informants: Letters, Interviews, and Statements about Abraham Lincoln* (Urbana: University of Illinois Press, 1998), 655.

8. Harding in Parkinson, "Patent Case," 116.

9. Ralph Emerson to the editor of *McClure's Magazine*, Chicago, 15 May 1896, Ida M. Tarbell Papers, Allegheny College.

10. Letter by Mary Manny Tinker, Rockford, Illinois, 21 [*sic*] July 1896, Rockford *Register-Gazette*, 20 July 1896.

11. John J. Duff, *A. Lincoln, Prairie Lawyer* (New York: Rinehart, 1960), 323; Donn Piatt in Benjamin P. Thomas and Harold M. Hyman, *Stanton: The Life and Times of Lincoln's Secretary of War* (New York: Alfred A. Knopf, 1962), 66.

12. William B. H. Dowse to Albert J. Beveridge, Boston, 16 October 1925, Beveridge Papers, Library of Congress. From 1878 to 1890, Dowse worked in Harding's New York office.

13. Harding told this story to Benjamin Rush Cowen. Cowen, *Abraham Lincoln: An Appreciation by One Who Knew Him* (Cincinnati: Robert Clarke, 1909), 10–12. Cf. George Alfred Townsend's interview with Harding, clipping marked "Globe 11–9-1909," Lincoln Museum, Fort Wayne, Indiana.

14. W. M. Dickson, "Abraham Lincoln at Cincinnati," *Harper's New Monthly Magazine* 69 (June 1884): 62.

15. Harding told this to his law partner William B. H. Dowse. Dowse to Albert J. Beveridge, Boston, 10 October 1925, Beveridge Papers, Library of Congress.

16. Report of a statement by Harding, n.d., typescript, Ida M. Tarbell Papers, Allegheny College.

17. Thomas and Hyman, *Stanton*, 136; Harding told this to Charles F. Benjamin, who in turn described it to Horace White. Benjamin to White, 1 June 1914, White Papers, Lincoln Presidential Library, Springfield. Benjamin had been a clerk in the war department during the Civil War.

18. Dawes, "Recollections of Stanton under Lincoln," *Atlantic Monthly*, April 1894, 163; Dawes, "Some Sayings of Mr. Lincoln," undated typescript, Dawes Papers, Library of Congress.

19. Washington correspondence, n.d., Philadelphia *Inquirer*, n.d., copied in the Boston *Evening Journal*, 22 January 1862.

20. Peter Cozzens and Robert I. Girardi, eds., *The Military Memoirs of General John Pope* (Chapel Hill: University of North Carolina Press, 1998), 115.

21. Glyndon G. Van Deusen, *William Henry Seward* (New York: Oxford University Press, 1967), 324.

22. Allan Nevins and Milton Halsey, eds., *The Diary of George Templeton Strong* (4 vols.; New York: Macmillan, 1952), 2:203 (entry for 29 January 1862).

23. Washington correspondence by "Van" [D. W. Bartlett], 15 January, Springfield, Massachusetts, *Republican*, 18 January 1862.

24. New York *Herald*, 15 January 1862.

25. Holt to Lincoln, St. Louis, 15 January 1862, Lincoln Papers, Library of Congress.

26. Edwards Pierrepont to Lincoln, New York, 19 January 1862, Lincoln Papers, Library of Congress.

27. Fernando Wood to Lincoln, New York, 15 January 1862, Lincoln Papers, Library of Congress.

28. Portland *Oregonian*, 20 May 1862.

29. Washington correspondence, 19 January, Philadelphia *Inquirer*, 20 January 1862.

30. Washington correspondence by James Brooks, 16 January, New York *Evening Express*, 17 January 1862.

31. New York *Tribune*, 21 January 1862.

32. Stanton to Dana, Washington, 24 January 1862, Dana Papers, Library of Congress.

33. Bernard A. Weisberger, *Reporters for the Union* (Boston: Little, Brown, 1953), 222–23.

34. Michael Burlingame, ed., *Lincoln's Journalist: John Hay's Anonymous Writings for the Press, 1860–1864* (Carbondale: Southern Illinois University Press, 1998), 196–97.

35. Howard K. Beale and Alan W. Brownsword, eds., *Diary of Gideon Welles, Secretary of the Navy under Lincoln and Johnson* (3 vols.; New York: W. W. Norton, 1960), 1: 56, 59.

36. Marvin R. Cain, *Lincoln's Attorney General: Edward Bates of Missouri* (Columbia: University of Missouri Press, 1965), 172; Beale and Brownsword, eds., *Diary of Gideon Welles*, 1:57.

37. McClellan, *McClellan's Own Story: The War for the Union* (New York: C. L. Webster, 1887), 152.

38. John Niven, *Gideon Welles: Lincoln's Secretary of the Navy* (New York: Oxford University Press, 1973), 397; Thomas and Hyman, *Stanton*, 128–30.

39. Joshua F. Speed to Joseph Holt, Washington, 4 February 1862, Holt Papers, Library of Congress.

40. Washington correspondence, 27 January, Philadelphia *Inquirer*, 28 January 1862.

41. Carpenter, *Six Months at the White House*, 245–46.

42. Cozzens and Girardi, eds., *Military Memoirs of Pope*, 115.

43. Hay to Stanton, Paris, 26 July 1865, in Michael Burlingame, ed., *At Lincoln's Side: John Hay's Civil War Correspondence and Selected Writings* (Carbondale: Southern Illinois University Press, 2000), 106.

8. LINCOLN AND GENERAL GEORGE B. MCCLELLAN

1. Michael Burlingame, *The Inner World of Abraham Lincoln* (Urbana: University of Illinois Press, 1994), 182; Stephen W. Sears, *Controversies and Commanders: Dispatches from the Army of the Potomac* (Boston: Houghton Mifflin, 1999), 13–14.

2. Michael Burlingame and John R. Turner Ettlinger, eds., *Inside Lincoln's White House: The Complete Civil War Diary of John Hay* (Carbondale: Southern Illinois University Press, 1997), 32 (entry for 13 November 1861).

3. William H. Russell, *My Diary North and South* (Boston: T.O.H.P. Burnham, 1863), 552 (entry for 9 October 1861).

4. Comte de Paris diary, 28 September 1861, in Russell H. Beatie, *Army of the Potomac: Birth of Command, November 1860–September 1861* (New York: Da Capo, 2002), 1:488–89.

5. John M. Wilson, then a lieutenant on McClellan's staff, in the Brooklyn *Eagle*, 12 February 1913.

6. David Dixon Porter, "Journal of Occurrences during the War of the Rebellion," 1:173–74, Porter Papers, Library of Congress.

7. Memorandum by C. C. Buel, New York, 23 November 1885 (recalling the words uttered the previous evening by Horace Porter), Richard Watson Gilder Papers, New York Public Library.

8. F. A. Mitchell to John Hay, East Orange, New Jersey, 3 January 1889, Nicolay-Hay Papers, Lincoln Presidential Library, Springfield.

9. William O. Stoddard, *Inside the White House in War Times: Memoirs and Reports of Lincoln's Secretary*, ed. Michael Burlingame (1890; Lincoln: University of Nebraska Press, 2000), 63.

10. In 1869 Burnside told this story at a dinner party in London. Manuscript diary of Benjamin Moran, Library of Congress (entry for 11 December 1869).

11. This occurred on the afternoon of December 15. Mark De Wolf Howe, *The Life and Letters of George Bancroft* (2 vols.; New York: C. Scribner's Sons, 1908), 2:246–47.

12. Stephen W. Sears, *George B. McClellan: The Young Napoleon* (New York: Ticknor & Fields, 1988), 59.

13. Stephen W. Sears, ed., *The Civil War Papers of George B. McClellan: Selected Correspondence, 1860–1865* (New York: Ticknor & Fields, 1989), 323.

14. Theodore Calvin Pease and James G. Randall, eds., *The Diary of Orville Hickman Browning* (2 vols.; Springfield: Illinois State Historical Library, 1925–33), 1:559 (entry for 14 July 1862).

9. REMOVAL OF MCCLELLAN FROM COMMAND: NOVEMBER 1862

1. Michael Burlingame and John R. Turner Ettlinger, eds., *Inside Lincoln's White House: The Complete Civil War Diary of John Hay* (Carbondale: Southern Illinois University Press, 1997), 62 (entry for 14 July 1863).

2. Washington correspondence, 3 November, New York *Tribune*, 9 November 1862.

3. Lincoln said this to Ozias M. Hatch. Hatch interviewed by John G. Nicolay, Springfield, June 1875, in Michael Burlingame, ed., *An Oral History of Abraham Lincoln: John G. Nicolay's Interviews and Essays* (Carbondale: Southern Illinois University Press, 1996), 16.

4. T. J. Barnett to S. L. M. Barlow, Washington, 23 September 1862, Barlow Papers, Huntington Library, San Marino, California.

5. William M. Dickson "A Leaf from the Unwritten History of the Rebellion," draft, Dickson Papers, University of Michigan. Key made a similar statement to Nathaniel Paige of the New York *Tribune*. New York *Tribune*, n.d., copied in an undated, unidentified clipping, Lincoln Museum, Fort Wayne, Indiana.

6. McClellan to Mary Ellen McClellan, Sharpsburg, Maryland, 5 October 1862, in Stephen W. Sears, ed., *The Civil War Papers of George B. McClellan: Selected Correspondence, 1860–1865* (New York: Ticknor & Fields, 1989), 490.

7. Washington correspondence by "Van" [D. W. Bartlett], 7 October, Springfield (Mass.) *Republican*, 11 October 1862. Bartlett's source was a member of the presidential entourage.

8. Lincoln told this to David Davis. David Davis to Leonard Swett, Washington, 26 November 1862, David Davis Papers, Lincoln Presidential Library.

9. *Spirit of the Times* (New York), n.d., copied in the Cincinnati *Commercial*, 24 October 1862.

10. Washington correspondence by "Van" [D. W. Bartlett], 21 October, Springfield (Massachusetts) *Republican*, 25 October 1862.

11. McClellan to Mary Ellen McClellan, Sharpsburg, Maryland, 2 October 1862, in Sears, ed., *Civil War Papers of McClellan,* 488.

12. Hatch interviewed by John G. Nicolay, Springfield, June 1875, in Burlingame, ed., *Oral History of Lincoln*, 16.

13. Sharpsburg correspondence, 3 October, New York *Times*, 12 October 1862; Theodore Calvin Pease and James G. Randall, eds., *The Diary of Orville Hickman Browning* (2 vols.; Springfield: Illinois State Historical Library, 1925–33), 1:594–95 (entry for 12 December 1862).

14. Du Pont to his wife, Washington, 16 October 1862, and at sea aboard the *Keystone*, 10, 21 October 1862; and to Henry Winter Davis, 25 October 1862, all in John D. Hayes, ed., *Samuel Francis Du Pont: A Selection from His Civil War Letters* (3 vols.; Ithaca, N.Y.: Published for the Eleutherian Mills Historical Library by the Cornell University Press, 1969), 2:245–47, 251–53.

15. Benjamin Brown French, *Witness to the Young Republic: A Yankee's Journal, 1828–1870*, ed. Donald B. Cole and John J. McDonough (Hanover, N.H.: University Press of New England, 1989), 405 (entry for 3 August 1862).

16. Washington correspondence by "Van" [D. W. Bartlett], 17 December, Springfield (Massachusetts) *Republican*, 19 December 1862.

17. *The War of the Rebellion: A Compilation of the Official Records of the Union and Confederate Armies* (127 vols.; Washington: Government Printing Office, 1880–1900), series 1, vol. 19, part 1, p. 72.

18. Halleck to McClellan, Washington, 14 October 1862, *War of the Rebellion*, series 1, vol. 19, part 2, p. 421.

19. Lincoln to McClellan, Washington, 25 October 1862, in Roy P. Basler et al., eds., *The Collected Works of Abraham Lincoln* (8 vols. plus index; New Brunswick, N.J.: Rutgers University Press, 1953–55), 5:474.

20. Sears, ed., *Civil War Papers of McClellan,* 334. Meigs denied that McClellan reported accurately on the number of good horses available to him. Meigs to Stanton, Washington, 14 October 1862, Alexander Stewart Webb Papers, Yale University.

21. Lincoln to McClellan, Washington, 27 October 1862, Basler, ed., *Collected Works of Lincoln,* 5:479.

22. Nicolay to Therena Bates, Washington, 13 October 1862, in Burlingame, ed., *With Lincoln in the White House,* 89.

23. Lincoln to McClellan, Washington, 26 October 1862, Basler, ed., *Collected Works of Lincoln,* 5:477.

24. Basler, ed., *Collected Works of Lincoln,* 5:460–61

25. *War of the Rebellion,* series 1, vol. 19, part 1, p. 81.

26. Burlingame, ed., *With Lincoln in the White House,* 90.

27. McClellan to Mary Ellen McClellan, Berlin, ca. 29 October 1862, Sears, ed., *Civil War Papers of McClellan,* 515.

28. Adams S. Hill reporting what Lincoln told General James S. Wadsworth, in Hill to Sydney Howard Gay, 13 October 1862, Gay Papers, Columbia University, in Don E. Fehrenbacher and Virginia Fehrenbacher, eds., *Recollected Words of Abraham Lincoln* (Stanford, Calif.: Stanford University Press, 1996), 458.

29. Washington correspondence, 3 November, New York *Tribune,* 9 November 1862.

30. Nicolay to Therena Bates, Washington, 9 November 1862, in Burlingame, ed., *With Lincoln in the White House,* 90–91.

31. Joseph L. Maguire to N. P. Banks, New York, 11 November 1862, Banks Papers, Library of Congress.

32. Francis P. Blair Sr. to Francis P. Blair Jr., 7 November 1862; Francis P. Blair Sr. to Montgomery Blair, 2 March 1863, Blair Family Papers, Library of Congress.

33. J. G. Barnard to [John Sherman], Washington, 6 January 1863 [misdated 1862], John Sherman Papers, Library of Congress.

34. Pease and Randall, eds., *Browning Diary,* 1:589–90 (entry for 29 November 1862).

35. Burlingame and Ettlinger, eds., *Hay Diary,* 232 (entry for 25 September 1864).

36. Sears, *Young Napoleon,* 339.

10. CABINET CRISIS: DECEMBER 1862

1. *Harpers Weekly,* 27 December 1862.

2. Benjamin Brown French, *Witness to the Young Republic: A Yankee's Journal, 1828–1870,* ed. Donald B. Cole and John J. McDonough (Hanover, N.H.: University Press of New England, 1989), 415 (entry for 21 December 1862).

3. Allan Nevins and Milton Halsey Thomas, eds., *The Diary of George Templeton Strong* (4 vols.; New York: Macmillan, 1952), 3:281–82 (entry for 18 December 1862).

4. Charles Eliot Norton to George William Curtis, Shady Hill, 12 November 1862, *Letters of Charles Eliot Norton,* ed. Sara Norton and M. A. De Wolfe Howe (2 vols.; Boston: Houghton Mifflin, 1913), 1:258.

5. James [Hill?] to Edward McPherson, Chambersburg, Pennsylvania, 19 December 1862; [R. G. McCreary?] to Edward McPherson, Gettysburg, Pennsylvania, 17 December 1862, Edward McPherson Papers, Library of Congress.

6. Brownson to Sumner, 26 December 1862, in David Donald, *Charles Sumner and the Rights of Man* (New York: Knopf, 1970), 89.

7. Jay to Sumner, 18 December 1862, in Donald, *Charles Sumner,* 89.

8. George F. Williams to Sumner, 17 December 1862, in Donald, *Charles Sumner,* 89.

9. Allen Thorndike Rice, ed., *Reminiscences of Abraham Lincoln, by Distinguished Men of His Time* (New York: North American, 1886), 276.

10. Chandler to his wife, Washington, 18 December 1862, Chandler Papers, Library of Congress; Chandler to Lyman Trumbull, Detroit, 10 September 1862, Lyman Trumbull Papers, Library of Congress.

11. James Alexander Hamilton, *Reminiscences of James A. Hamilton; or, Men and Events, at Home and Abroad, during Three Quarters of a Century* (New York: C. Scribner & Co., 1869), 529–30.

12. Thaddeus Stevens to Simon Stevens, Lancaster, Pennsylvania, 19 November 1862, in Beverly Wilson Palmer, ed., *The Selected Papers of Thaddeus Stevens* (2 vols.; Pittsburgh: University of Pittsburgh Press, 1997–98), 1: 328.

13. Theodore Calvin Pease and James G. Randall, eds., *The Diary of Orville Hickman Browning* (2 vols.; Springfield: Illinois State Historical Library, 1925–33), 1:597–99 (entries for 16 and 17 December 1862); Francis Fessenden, *Life and Public Services of William Pitt Fessenden (*2 vols.; Boston: Houghton, Mifflin, 1907), 1:232–38.

14. David Herbert Donald, *"We Are Lincoln Men": Abraham Lincoln and His Friends* (New York: Simon & Schuster, 2003), 140–176; Glyndon G. Van Deusen, *William Henry Seward* (New York: Oxford University Press, 1967), 335–48.

15. Howard K. Beale and Alan W. Brownsword, eds., *Diary of Gideon Welles, Secretary of the Navy under Lincoln and Johnson* (3 vols.; New York: W. W. Norton, 1960), 1:203, 205.

16. Frank Blair to his father, n.d., Blair-Lee Papers, Princeton University.

17. John Niven, *Salmon P. Chase: A Biography* (New York: Oxford University Press, 1995), 310; Chase to Zachariah Chandler, Washington, 20 September 1862, *The Salmon P. Chase Papers,* ed. John Niven et al. (5 vols.; Kent, Ohio: Kent State University Press, 1993–98), 2:275–76. Cf. Chase to John Sherman, Washington, 20 September 1862, *ibid.,* 2:277–78.

18. Washington correspondence by Agate [Whitelaw Reid], 20 December, Cincinnati *Gazette*, 23 December 1862.

19. Pease and Randall, eds., *Diary of Orville Hickman Browning*, 1:602 (entry for 19 December 1862).

11. LINCOLN'S FAME

1. Hans L. Trefousse, *First among Equals: Abraham Lincoln's Reputation during His Administration* (New York: Fordham University Press, 2005).

2. Count S. Stakelberg, "Tolstoi Holds Lincoln World's Greatest Hero," New York *World*, 7 February 1909.

INDEX

MICHAEL BURLINGAME, Sadowski Professor of History Emeritus at Connecticut College, is the author of *The Inner World of Abraham Lincoln* and the editor of ten volumes of Lincoln primary source materials, including *An Oral History of Abraham Lincoln: John G. Nicolay's Interviews and Essays*; *With Lincoln in the White House: Letters, Memoranda, and Other Writings of John G. Nicolay*; *Lincoln's Journalist: John Hay's Anonymous Writings for the Press, 1860–1864*; *At Lincoln's Side: John Hay's Civil War Correspondence and Selected Writings*; and, with John R. Turner Ettlinger, *Inside Lincoln's White House: The Complete Civil War Diary of John Hay*, all published by Southern Illinois University Press. He is currently working on a four-volume life of Lincoln.